Scrabble in the Afternoon

Biddy Wells lives in west Wales. She is passionate about her writing. She walks daily and loves nature, especially the Pembrokeshire coast and hills. She has two grown-up children and adores her relatively new role of grandmother. She enjoys travelling, particularly overland around Europe, and she always loves to come home to Wales. Her first memoir, *A Van of One's Own*, was a best-seller and continues to strike a chord with readers.

Scrabble in the Afternoon

Biddy Wells

PARTHIAN

Parthian, Cardigan SA43 1ED
www.parthianbooks.com
First published in 2021

ISBN 978-1-912109-30-2
Ebook ISBN 978-1-912681-91-4
Edited by Carly Holmes
Cover design www.theundercard.co.uk
Cover image by Biddy Wells
Typeset by Elaine Sharples
Printed by 4edge Ltd, UK
Published with the financial support of the Welsh Books Council
British Library Cataloguing in Publication Data
A cataloguing record for this book is available from the British Library.

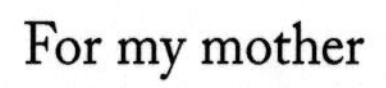
For my mother

Part One

It was the first of January. I followed the ambulance for an hour. I wouldn't let anyone get between me and the speeding vehicle, even at roundabouts I drove so close that I imagined anyone could see an umbilical cord connected us, and I was not to be trifled with. Slightly hysterical sacred music boomed out of the speakers, an extraordinary jazz/funk mass I'd recently bought on CD. Altos chanted and sopranos soared. I picked out words: Sanctus; Angus Dei; Gloria; Kyrie Eleison. It was a little surreal but entirely appropriate.

Though I was swimming with adrenaline, I felt completely calm. Only a short while before I had been holding my mother's head up to keep her airways open. All signs of life had gone. She was slumped in a chair, her arms dangling and twitching, her skin clammy. She was deathly pale and had no pulse that I could detect. Her eyes were wide open, senselessly staring at nothing. Could she hear me? I didn't think so. Just before she lost consciousness she'd said, 'It's as though you're far, far away...'

I knew I had to get her into a horizontal position, but it was impossible. A substantial woman, she'd lost the strength in her legs some years before and now she was a dead weight. Moving her would have been highly risky. I held her head up with one hand; in the other was the phone. A woman I will never meet coached me, telling me I was doing really well. She stayed on the line for half an hour or so while we waited for the ambulance.

All this time, Mum was unconscious but still breathing – just. I saw how the body looks when life leaves it. The expression in her eyes – the absence of it. These were not Mum's eyes. I'd thought she might be dead, or in the process of dying peacefully right in front of me. I spoke softly and comfortingly to her and listened to the kindly, nameless woman who stayed on the phone supporting me.

It occurred to me that this was perfect. This was exactly how she would have wanted to go: I was by her side, holding her and witnessing her tranquil passing from this long life to the next.

Time slowed down and became meaningless. After a while, astonishingly, Mum came round to find herself lying on her bed surrounded by two paramedics and two ambulance men in bright orange uniforms. Alarmed, she tried to speak but her words came out as a stream of scrambled, incomprehensible syllables.

It took a while to calm her and it was a struggle to get her down the stairs strapped to a chair. I remember thinking that if she survived this she would have no speech or movement. For her that would be a fate worse than death.

A week before, I had been excited because for the first time in years we were all going to be together – almost my whole family. I was delighted that things seemed to be falling into place. My brother would collect Mum on his way and bring her to my house which was newly vacant. Normally I rented it out as I no longer lived there. We would all be able to stay for a couple of days and enjoy the log fire.

But then Mum rang me and said she didn't feel up to it. She couldn't face the journey and not having all the things she needed: the stair-lift; the bath-hoist; the grab-handles; the wheeled trolleys; the raised seats and bed. I understood. It would have been hard for her. We made a plan B: my brother would stay with her on Christmas Eve and drive over in time for our family lunch next day. Mum really didn't mind missing Christmas she said. She preferred it this way.

My partner, David, and I had been looking forward to a rest. It had been a tough autumn. It had rained for approximately eighty days consecutively and there had been gales. We'd got used to the weather, battened down the hatches and given up hoping for blue sky. Both of us had been ill with a variety of bugs that had been doing the rounds. We'd recovered, but both longed for a break – which would fit neatly into the week between Christmas and New Year – when we could do nothing, and please no-one but ourselves. On the horizon was our planned three-month trip to Portugal. I could hardly wait.

In the run up to Christmas Mum had been stressed. This was not unusual; she often talked of her 'anxiety complex' whilst insisting that she was doing well, living alone with her disability which meant she could get around only with the help of her wheelie-walker, and other mobility aids. She liked her own company and immersed herself in writing, crosswords, and afternoons on the sofa watching snooker on TV. She had always been a stoic who wouldn't consider calling the doctor.

We rang Mum on Christmas day and she admitted she felt unwell but insisted we stay away and enjoy our lunch. The next morning she was worse, so I drove an hour east to her house to take care of her.

Boxing Day is not a good time to get hold of a doctor and it was days before her own GP came to see her. It turned out she had a very severe case of shingles, and it might take at least six weeks before she would recover her strength. She was extremely weak, in a lot of pain, and had no appetite. I stayed with her, waving goodbye to the restful week I'd longed for, and abandoning David who remained alone at my house and kept the place warm.

Mum rested in her bed, took anti-viral medication and painkillers, and ate the chicken broth I made her, along with tiny morsels of fruit. It soon became obvious that she would have to come home with me, so that I could care for her until the shingles subsided. She agreed to my plan and resolved to muster enough strength to make the journey at the turn of the year.

By New Year's Day she was packed and ready to come down in the stair-lift for the first time in a week. As I entered her room she was sitting on her chair saying she felt faint. That was when she collapsed and my voice no longer reached her. That was when I dialled 999 and tried to steady myself as I spoke.

By the time the ambulance got her into A&E she was talking a little more coherently. They did all their tests but couldn't tell us anything. They kept her in for a night, then rang me to say that they were discharging her. 'Is there someone to look after her at home?' they asked. I gave them my address and waited.

Several hours passed. I rang the hospital, just over an hour's drive from my house, and they told me my mother had left in an ambulance hours earlier. I didn't know where she had got to and I started to feel more than a little anxious. It was a cold January day and my poor vulnerable mum was out there somewhere without a coat. The cord between us was tugging.

At last, Mum was carried up my front steps and gently bundled onto the spare bed that David had raised using four moss-covered breeze blocks he'd found in the garden. She smiled weakly and fell asleep. The ambulance, it transpired, had been on a scenic tour of west Wales so that an elderly gentleman could be taken home en route to my village. Unfortunately, he had forgotten where he lived.

I had imagined a state-of-the-art vehicle in which my mother would be wrapped up on a bed with a nurse holding her hand. In reality, the hospital had sent Mum home, wearing a nightie, on a draughty old hospital bus.

❧

'And how are *you* doing?' asked Dr Thomas. We had been discussing my mother and what might have happened to her. I was touched and a little thrown by his question about me. How *was* I doing? I was okay, I thought. It was hard to tell.

He was mystified: the cause of Mum's collapse remained unclear, though he suggested it could have been a mini stroke. I hadn't answered his question. Not out loud anyway. My life had changed overnight. One day I had been free of responsibility, about to go off travelling; the next I'd had to cancel everything, move back into the house I hadn't lived in for several years, and take in my mum so that I could give her round-the-clock care. This was a world I had heard about but never really entered, and though I'd known this day might eventually come, it was always far off in some distant future. After a while I told the doctor: 'I am fine, just fine.'

❧

After her second husband died, though she missed him, Mum excelled at living alone. I had often marvelled at her ability to exist – and even thrive – in her own small world. She was happy and independent. Though becoming increasingly disabled, she carried on alone having witnessed the departure of many loved ones, including her second son and most of her friends. 'I'm the last one standing,' she'd say without self-pity or even any observable emotion. Loss had been a major theme in her life and she seemed resilient almost to the point of indifference. Perhaps her stoicism was a shield that protected her from the fear and sadness that might have destroyed a more fragile personality.

Over the previous few years I'd started to notice that things were getting tougher for her, and my brother and I had talked about how the situation might have to change. It's hard to know when to intervene in someone else's life. We agreed that threatening Mum's independence would be a difficult and sad task. Would she agree to live in some kind of sheltered accommodation, or a care home? Whatever happened, it was going to be a one-way street; the end of an era and the beginning of a steeper decline, perhaps.

Life took care of it all. Suddenly decisions had to be made extremely quickly, and I was the obvious choice: the one who would scoop her up and take care of her. My brother lives several hours away and travels the world with his work, and he's not the type of person who could give things up to look after a parent. Was I that sort of person? I wondered. And did I have a choice?

My mother has always been pragmatic about her life – and about death. She would say 'Just stick me in a home', or 'I've had my life, you must have yours.' And she was being straight. She truly meant it. She would talk of death as something she positively welcomed. Not because she was suffering, or morbidly depressed, but because she had no fear of it. She believed that when she died she would enter another realm, experiencing things through a new, expanded perception. It would be pretty cosmic. There, she would be at one with her loved ones who had already made the mysterious transition into the Great Unknown.

But she hadn't died. She had gone somewhere and returned. She was profoundly weakened, ill, and sure that death would follow soon. She surrendered. All anxiety vanished and she allowed herself to be helpless.

After the first few days David had gone back to his own place in Pembrokeshire where we'd been living together for the previous few years. He said he'd come and see me the following weekend. For a week or so, while Mum spent most of the time sleeping, I spent hours each day on the phone waiting in queues and talking with nurses, social workers and the Department for Work and Pensions. I had to learn to understand their language and systems very quickly. I needed help and advice. Amongst other things we needed a wheelchair and a ramp to enable Mum to get out if there was a fire, or to get her into the car for the medical appointments that were sure to follow – though any ideas of her going beyond the threshold of her room any time soon seemed entirely unrealistic.

Social Services promised to sort out a care package. Help was on its way, apparently. My brother visited and brought some more of Mum's things from her house. For short periods she sat up in bed propped up by a mound of pillows, but mostly she slept. Sometimes I would sit at my desk staring out over the valley, trying to think. A blue woollen blanket was always wrapped around me as I couldn't get the house warm enough. Mum's room was a cosy boudoir with an electric radiator on all the time. When I went in to sit with her, I could feel myself thaw a little.

I couldn't help thinking about the future. What about getting out and doing things? What about the life I had assumed would continue? I was missing Pembrokeshire and my life with David. I wondered how he felt about my sudden departure, and what effect it might have on our relationship. I considered our forthcoming trip abroad. What if we couldn't go?

A mild rush of fear coursed through me daily. I stopped thinking and tried to stay right in the present moment. I made soup, and juiced a load of vegetables. I talked gently with Mum. Miraculously, her brain had survived and here she was: physically incapable, dependent on me for just about everything, but mentally, quite bright.

Mum's mind was remarkably busy. I took her a cup of tea one morning and she started chattering. I was sleepy, barely able to string a sentence together. I held up my hand in a gentle gesture and smiled. 'Sacred tea ceremony,' I mumbled through a yawn, and she laughed.

'Ah yes, I remember now,' she said. 'Sorry!' Then, with a hint of a wink, she made a *namaste* pose with her hands, palms together, and I left her to it. This was my time to sit for a few minutes, mug in hand, and stare into the middle distance.

There was a postcard on my bathroom wall that said: *With a cup of tea in one's hands, anything is possible*. How true that was. I was relieved that Mum had understood my need for quiet at this fragile time of day.

⁂

January continued, cold and grey. Now my mother and I seemed to be in competition, both coughing like a pair of life-long smokers. I would hear her across the hall. She had a long-running throat problem which affected swallowing and talking. I had a bug.

One day, I feared for a second that I might actually die, there and then in the hall, when I was supposed to be the carer – the one in charge and responsible for my mother. I couldn't catch my breath between coughing fits. I thought about the delicate thread between life and death. What would happen to my mother if I keeled over and died? I went to look for my jar of Vick's Vaporub.

⁂

One Sunday Mum announced, 'I'm going to do my space-walk now.' It was only her second voyage to the sitting room a few metres along the hall from her bedroom which she had dubbed her 'kennel'. She was feeling confident and looking forward to it. She managed well with her wheelie-walker, step by careful step. I followed close behind with the wheelchair in case she fell backwards.

Into my head popped: 'It's time to leave the capsule if you dare.' David Bowie had died recently, Mum surviving him by fourteen years. He was young, really, and he'd seemed immortal. I had feelings about his passing that I couldn't form into language, even if I hadn't been too tired to think.

⁂

Mum was hugely relieved that she no longer had to struggle on her own: coping, rather than living. The shingles seemed to be subsiding just a little. Each day she got out of bed, but not for long. Her clothes still hung on a rail – she hadn't got dressed since the previous year. The time we spent sitting together was generally uplifting. She was relaxed, sweet and grateful.

I had never imagined sharing a home with my mum. The idea would have filled me with a depressing dread. The image of a middle-aged woman living with her mother could have denoted some catastrophic failure on the part of the daughter. What sort of life could be blithely set aside in order to accommodate the full-time care of a parent? Certainly not a life of consequence or glamour. My life had neither to any great degree. I considered this not only convenient, but advantageous. I was able to drop everything because I had come to a point where, partly by design, I had a certain amount of freedom. And, of course, I cared about my mum because she was my mum. I loved her.

Yes, I could step into the breach – happily. I had just left my café job in order to tie up ends, pack up and go away with David. We could postpone our trip by a couple of months if necessary. It was a stroke of luck that just recently my house had been vacated so I could stay there with Mum while she recuperated. I was relieved that I didn't have to go and live at her house where I would be completely isolated from everyone and everything I knew.

But there were other things in the frame apart from practicalities. Things had not been easy between Mum and me in the past. I knew that there were deep, old feelings that I had tucked neatly away in a vault labelled: The Past: Do Not Open. Could I really live with my mother for more than just a few weeks? What were the chances of keeping the lid on things now that we were sharing a home?

❧

My parents married in the fifties and had two sons. They were switched-on thirty-somethings in the Swinging Sixties, when I was born, and they were navigating a world that was changing rapidly, even in small towns like ours in south Wales. In the seventies, reality continued to shift until the grey old, good old days slipped out of sight and out of reach. But there were remnants, customs that were cherished or that had sneaked, unexamined, into the new world. We'd all been trained to be seen and not heard. Nobody seemed to talk about anything that needed talking about. "Less said, the better" was a treasured motto.

We had a lovely house, we were not particularly poor and there was a vibrant social life that accompanied the competitive sailing scene for which my parents shared a passion that bordered on obsession. They sailed a lot and left me on a variety of beaches to look after myself. Presumably they thought these were safe and enjoyable places for a little girl to spend a few hours on Saturdays and Sundays. But I felt lonely, anxious and bored. On one occasion, when I was about six, I was saved from drowning by my mum's friend who had spotted me reaching out from a pier to try and catch my parents as they glided by, unaware. I fell into the murky sea and sank. Perhaps that single event coloured my thinking and created a terrible story of a miserable childhood. Perhaps it was the tip of a very real iceberg. It was certainly a telling metaphor.

My brothers loved sailing, but I grew to hate it because the sea had stolen my parents. I loved them and, really, I knew they loved me – Dad worked hard for our material comfort and Mum transformed housekeeping money into wonderful family dinners. They were witty, vibrant people. Our annual caravan holiday was perfect, and Christmases were wondrous. Yet they didn't seem all that interested in me. I felt neglected. Mostly, my needs were a nuisance. I learned early on that complaining was futile and unwelcome.

My mother adored both her sons but around the younger of my two older brothers she wove a protective cloak. She felt he needed to be defended from criticism. That might have felt suffocating, and irritating, but actually it seemed to embolden him. Being five years younger, and very low in the pecking order, I believed that I was in need of the sort of attention and protection that he got. I was not jealous, so much as vulnerable and insecure. I wasn't sure I was part of a pack which consisted of three strong, vociferous males and my mum, who saw herself as one of the boys. She would say, 'If you can't beat them, join them.' I wasn't able to join them.

Mum used to tell me that by the time I came along she had had enough of being a mother and that there was not much left for me. Though this didn't seem fair, I took it on the chin. It was simply a fact. Later in life I looked back and I wondered whether she had viewed me as competition, or whether she just got on better with boys than girls.

Despite their shared love of sailing there was disharmony in my parents' marriage. Mum was sorely disappointed that my father seemed to prefer other women to her, at least superficially. They were both capable of flirting with their friends, perhaps believing that I didn't notice – but I did notice, and it made me feel unsafe.

The marriage got rocky, cracked under the strain of various

infidelities, and came apart eventually after my brothers had left home. I was left alone in my early teenage years to witness my relatively familiar life unravel messily and turn into something that felt completely alien.

My father quickly re-married and Mum became more interested in finding a companion and fulfilling her romantic ambitions than in family life. This was understandable. Motherhood was a long-haul – a life-long commitment – and she had not secured the things she needed and expected from the whole deal. Also, her family was now just the three of us: her, my gran who lived with us, and me. Mum was relatively free and relatively lonely.

Frequently, she drew me in and made me her friend. We talked about all sorts of things. However, I could not depend on this friendship. I could not be sure if she was truly available to me, or predict whether or not she would stand in my corner. Perhaps I needed my mother to be something else, not a friend. I didn't know, at the time, about something called 'emotional holding'. I had not considered consistency. When I was a teenager it was convenient and rather cool to be granted complete freedom to stray away from home. Mum didn't seem to worry about me at all.

Whenever I revisited the story of my early life I felt I was reading between the lines, vaguely aware of things that I couldn't quite put my finger on. At the time all I knew was how I felt inside myself. I tended to trust my gut feeling and respond accordingly when possible, as my generation were encouraged to do. Despite her laissez-faire attitude towards my comings and goings my mother seemed to follow a strict set of principles about how certain things *should* be: I ought to think like this, or should not feel that, and if I did, I shouldn't express it. I wasn't sure where these rather cerebral ideas had come from, but Mum seemed certain they were correct. They were her rules and I was living under her roof.

I had to get through exams and make choices about what I would do next, but my springboard into adulthood had collapsed along with my parents' marriage. I knew I needed to get away and find somewhere I belonged. There was a long low point in our relationship that began around the time I left home and moved to England at sixteen. I lost my mother then. Initially the schism had happened partly by my own doing: once I had got free of the nest I realised that I needed to create my own world which would feel wholesome and be inhabited by people I liked and trusted. I needed to heal some wounds and sort myself out. My parents became peripheral characters. I didn't consciously shut them out, but I did make a safe haven for myself. I was not sure what they knew about me or my life. I expected very little from them and they didn't disappoint me.

We were getting on with our own lives. My gran died. Mum had met a new man she really loved and who loved her. When we did spend time together on my occasional visits, it led to disappointment. Mum expected that I should be not only off her hands, but also cheerful and self-sufficient. I put on a good show of managing my own life but in fact I was in turmoil and I still needed her in some way.

By chance my partner and I moved back to my home patch in my early twenties. I was pregnant and Mum and I became closer. She bonded with her first grandchild, helped out, and was still around two years later, when my son was born. Then things got sticky again. She was busy with other things and I felt overwhelmed and isolated. I had expectations that she would be more supportive than she was able or willing to be. Perhaps I failed to tell her how much I needed her for fear I might feel rejected. It felt as though she disappeared again.

Sometimes my mum admitted openly that she had not been a very good mother. I didn't think she was talking about her enjoyment of gin or the fact that she smoked at the breakfast table, she knew she had been remiss in a more fundamental way. As was typical of her, she easily confessed her "sins". She would chuckle and say 'Oh I was a terrible mother... absolutely dreadful... probably rather careless.' Perhaps she was being candid and showing humility, or maybe she was joking. but to me it wasn't all that funny – she didn't seem to appreciate the gravity or the lasting effect her shortcomings had had on me. To her it was all in a day's work. I had the feeling she had very little idea or interest in how I felt about her as a mother. We didn't talk about that much. I harboured a lot of sadness and resentment, but I couldn't find a way to speak candidly about was going on inside me. I didn't think she could hear me. We simply didn't connect.

As time went on we continued to maintain a safe distance for the most part – both of us guarding something – both of us aware that less is more. Elephants in the room were ignored. There were things that I knew instinctively I wasn't allowed to say, and things she preferred not to think about or didn't want to discuss. There were whole chunks of our life that she claimed she couldn't remember at all. Still, we were friendly. We played Scrabble or did crosswords. We drank gin and made each other laugh. Having found a vehicle that worked for us, we avoided the tricky stuff and glided on a flyover that took us efficiently and pleasantly from the beginning to the end of visits. Even so, I knew that I could only be around her for a few hours at a time, and not too often. Perhaps she felt the same.

Now here I was back in the fold, back in the orbit and gravitational pull of my mother. For now, I had to sacrifice myself and my hard-won life to look after a woman who had not looked after me as I would have liked her to. It felt horribly mean-spirited to admit this but it was simply the truth – clearly, I had my own 'shoulds' about mothering – for Mum to hold onto some independence I had to forgo mine at least until she got better. I decided to give it my best shot: put old resentments aside for now and care for her to the best of my ability and with a willing heart. For a while she could rest and recover in the peace and quiet of my house. I could give her sanctuary.

After a few weeks it started to dawn on me that this new situation was not so much a short interval as a complete change of circumstances that would continue until I did something to alter it. Settling her back in her house was not an option. Could I really just stick her in an old folks' home once she was back on her feet, so to speak? This didn't seem so simple now that I was facing it as a real possibility.

Mum was vulnerable and recovering slowly from serious illness. An upheaval would be stressful and would most likely set her back. She wouldn't thrive in an institution, with its strange surroundings, among unfamiliar people. She would be a fish out of water. She needed to live according to her inner barometer rather than fitting into rigid timetables and alien routines. I knew her well. Her need for freedom was still intact. It was part of her – a part I admired and respected. She needed me now – genuinely – to protect her. But how long would this go on and where did it leave me?

Increasingly, Mum appeared to be doing better than me. I felt like a wreck and my body was screaming at me, but she was gradually gaining strength and independence in miniscule increments. She started to walk to the bathroom alone with her wheels and managed, though it was an effort, to wash by herself.

It had been cloudy for weeks. Smoke curled from the chimneys of the houses whose rooftops appeared just below eye-level when I sat at my desk; beyond them stood the wooded hill. It wasn't a bad view – it wasn't a bad place. Although rather unusual and decidedly dilapidated, my house was familiar and homely. I was unexpectedly resident back in a place I had left years ago.

Each day all I had to do was follow the protocol – the one I'd made up – which seemed to suit both of us well. After breakfast, I worked through the day's long list of tasks. I had no choice but to keep going. My mother's life depended on me just as mine has once depended on her.

Phone calls took up a lot of time in that first month or so and normally they led to frustration. I had the hospital telling me that I really must get Mum to Outpatients for tests to investigate her unconscious episode. At the same time Social Services proved very unhelpful regarding providing a ramp for the wheelchair. They talked of grants, surveyors, means-testing and a hideous concrete construction that would ruin my slate steps. It would all take time. Meanwhile if there was a fire Mum would be trapped. The Outpatients Department didn't know about the steps and Mum didn't care about the appointment. 'Let them go hang,' she said, laughing. She was serene in those early weeks. It was if she'd already arrived in heaven.

'The food's excellent here,' she said with a grin, one afternoon. 'You've got a good chef.' Her appetite had returned. Her taste was a little on the discerning side, but she was grateful. All she had to do was relax and be helped and fed. I hadn't realised how stressful it had been for her all those years living alone. She was always worried about falling, and always in pain.

Her life before her collapse had been limited and simple enough, and now she found herself confined to just one small bedroom in my house, yet she was never bored. She was thrilled to make an occasional trip to the bathroom so that I could give her a shower. For her, this was an exhausting upheaval but it made her feel as though she'd spent an afternoon in a luxury spa.

It seemed she had let go of something – come to a place of acceptance. I couldn't remember her being like this before. Her positive, pragmatic approach was infectious and it was an unexpected joy to help her. This was partly thanks to the fact that she hadn't suffered any cognitive damage despite being unconscious for so long, so we were able to discuss philosophical things, not just small-talk – that would have driven me nuts.

I was not earning anything, but it didn't seem to matter. Like Mum, I wasn't going anywhere, and we were managing the bills and living very simply, one day at a time. There was a sense that we were both letting go and coming to accept this situation. Life outside in "the real world" did not impinge on the quiet attention being lavished on minutiae, and the efficient, steady management of practicalities. Some days life began to feel almost like a meditation. However, even in this state of relative timelessness, the weekends seemed to come round quicker than ever before. Time was flying by alarmingly swiftly. This was odd; after all, I wasn't exactly having fun.

One Saturday David built a wooden ramp that swept over the front steps. It was magnificent and better than anything I could imagine Social Services would have come up with. This spelled freedom for Mum: she'd be able to sit in the garden when spring arrived, which was something I couldn't help thinking might never happen. The wild stormy weather looked set to continue and Mum said, 'I think the world might be coming to an end, literally.' She listened to the news and weather forecast religiously, a habit she refused to give up even though she agreed that it was utterly depressing.

David said that it was time to start being a little more proactive about getting a bit of help. Perhaps someone could come and sit with Mum for a few hours so that I could have a break, he suggested. I made some calls. There didn't seem to be any help available.

❧

One evening Mum and I were talking about death – one of her favourite subjects. She was worn out after the weekend when my brother had visited again. She'd found it 'over-stimulating', talking and thinking about the future. My brother urged us to face the issue of how we were going to manage financially, and how we were going to deal with the possible selling or renting of the house that Mum had lived in for over a decade. Now it had become a useless drain on her meagre resources. This was a big subject, and one that I had put aside. In truth I couldn't see Mum ever going back to living alone. That meant I could be looking after her for the long term. And that brought us back to death. 'I won't live long. I'm not worried and I'm ready to go,' she said with a beatific half-smile. She seemed to truly believe that her time was up. I wasn't so sure.

After a while I realised I was absolutely exhausted. It was the sheer continuousness of it all: breakfast, lunch and supper, popping down to the shops, laundry, bathing, brushing Mum's long, silver hair, keeping her company and organising repairs to my house. Then there were the medical appointments, the phone calls, the interactions with agencies that are supposed to be there to help, but whose systems I could never understand. Mum noticed I was becoming weary and tried to demand as little as possible. It was not her fault. It was not anybody's fault.

For most of the time we were one another's only companion. I stayed with her in the afternoons while she sat up in bed, and we talked about life and death in general terms. We had always found common ground on certain crucial, yet impersonal, topics. We were similar because of heredity, genes and nurture – that was obvious. But we were very different too. I had moved along a path that led me away from my family's culture and values. I had become very much my own person, and I had strong ideas about how to live and thrive and grow. I wanted to share them. But: 'You're befuddling me! I don't have room in my head for all these crazy ideas,' she'd say and we could venture no further.

I suspect I had hidden away a part of myself that harboured a fantasy version of my relationship with my parents. That part belonged to a small child that I could remember but had left behind. As a child I knew, though I had no words to explain it, that I had arrived in a world that was all wrong, and in which I didn't belong. I was the odd one out who was unwilling to cooperate with a system I found unfathomable and/or unacceptable.

As I matured, I forgot about my findings or filed them away under "childish idealism" or "naivety". The idealism didn't die, it just hid while I grew into a shape that was expected of me, and I guess I became all wrong myself. Things changed over time. I started to consider notions like personal growth, feminism, empowerment, healing, and spirituality. Earnestly, I sought truth and meaning, whatever those words meant. Thanks partly to a long spell in therapy, I came to terms with myself, and found a way to live in peace with life.

Now an unexpected possibility had arisen: Mum, at eighty-three, and I, thirty years younger, were at the edge of an opportunity to try a new way of being after a long life of behaving habitually, conforming to our familial roles and relying on "old thinking".

Although I hadn't chosen this situation, I was optimistic about what it might have to offer us. I hoped this time together would be harmonious and healing. I wanted us to be real and honest – *present* together – while we had the chance. That was quite a lot to ask of life, but now it felt possible. She had left her home: the place that housed and nurtured her habits. She was living under *my* roof now.

❧

February was hanging on by the skin of its teeth. Day after day monochrome clouds tumbled across the sky, driven by gale-force winds. My life had shrunk to a very limited palette of repetitive tasks and it could feel very dull. I was trying not to fight with my new reality but I kept returning to the question: How long will this go on? The thought sent a shudder through me.

Had things been different, David and I would have been on our way to Portugal. I didn't mind postponing our trip, but I was beginning to see that I might not be able to stray far from my mother for a long, long time. Mum could live for a decade or more, whatever she believed. And, of course, I wished her a long and happy life – but what about the next ten years of *my* life?

Since Mum entered her fifties death had been a constant threat for no rational reason. She'd been very comfortable with the idea, saying that she could 'go at the drop of a hat'. She seemed rather cavalier about her demise, laughing in its face, goading it to come and have a pop at her. Now she was expecting it to happen any minute. A watched kettle never boils.

David visited at weekends. With him, I could relax and feel truly comfortable. I didn't have to try to be anything for him and it was easy to understand him, mostly. I had little choice but to rely on him for help with practicalities and moral support. He seemed to be adapting to the change to our lifestyle with patience and good grace. My appreciation of him was growing by the day but I worried that he felt burdened under the pressure of being needed, of being the provider not just of practical help but also of the intimacy that compensated me for stresses I felt but couldn't explain even to myself.

⁂

Mum brought up the subject of death again: 'It's not that I'm not afraid of dying,' she said matter-of-factly. 'But I'm thinking about Judgement Day and I'm worried about not going to the right place.' This surprised me because we'd been discussing the great mystery of it all in our afternoon chats and I thought we had reached a nice tidy conclusion – all done and dusted.

We had agreed that we couldn't possibly know what would happen, and maybe *nothing* would happen. We might not see or hear or feel, so to all intents and purposes we will have been switched off.

'I think we simply join the great void, dissolving into a huge energy field,' she had said wistfully, only days before. She had held her hands aloft and marvelled. 'Perhaps we will gain a more expanded ability to comprehend how the entire universe works.' I had enjoyed our spirited conversations and couldn't remember them having included anything about a judgemental deity or hell.

Death, the most incredible and unknowable certainty of our existence, was something that Mum felt was about to happen to her, and she was facing up to it squarely. Serenity had come and enfolded her. She allowed herself to settle into the embrace of a very good mattress and the care of her loved ones (well, me). Despite her worries about her ultimate destination she had surrendered. It was good to be around her when she was in this state of just *being* and was no longer struggling to manage, nor addled about the past and the future. It was one long peaceful moment.

One Sunday there was a break in the cloud. I stirred David. We had till midday to do some outdoor jobs before heavy rain was forecast to start yet again. We cleared and swept, shovelled and scraped. A small area was now ready for Mum to sit in her wheelchair when the sun shone – *if* the sun ever shone again.

In the middle of all this wild weather I was experiencing my own internal turbulence. I recognised that it would not be a good idea to wish this time away so I tried to be patient. I was in the middle of the storm that is the menopause. Nights were incredible. Each was a voyage through a sea of sweats. I was drowning, gasping for air. I'd wake fighting my way out of the duvet as if it was smothering or strangling me. I found myself thrashing to get free, and then lying there in the freezing night air of my winter bedroom, completely drenched in sweat, exhausted, panting, shaking – my heart pounding – and feeling as though I'd been beaten up and thrown to the sea, my body washed up on an inhospitable rocky shore, shipwrecked.

Sometimes all this was accompanied by a weird, psychologically disturbing dream. I couldn't remember ever being breathless like this… Oh yes, actually I could. But those breathless nights of pleasure were long ago and far away. Then I had felt content, peaceful and satisfied. How cruel to be taken back to memories of a life that seemed to be all but over and certainly unavailable to me at the moment.

I must have been right in the epicentre of menopause and I couldn't imagine it getting any worse. During his weekend visits David slept through all this, despite the fact that he had all the winter bedclothes piled up on top of him. He just snored on through. Just as well.

⁂

Things started falling into place. We applied for financial assistance which, we discovered, Mum could have had years before. She was shocked – and so was I – when we realised just how long she had been “managing”, which was apparently code for “struggling”. Mum hadn’t received the right information and so she had never pursued the funding that could have helped her get a cleaner and even someone to help her occasionally with shopping.

One of the make-do-and-mend generation, she’d ironed paper bags, saved rubber bands, darned threadbare socks, and tailored her dresses and her desires according to what was available.

I remember an occasion long ago, when Mum had moved into a small, rented cottage. She was pretty hard up at the time and seemed to be enjoying the challenge of coming up with money-saving ideas. ‘Come and see this,’ she said proudly when I went to see her new home. She led me into the tiny back yard and pointed towards the ground. ‘I couldn’t afford gravel,’ she said, ‘but I needed to put something down to walk on, especially now that summer’s here. Look, they’re cockle shells! I got them free from the market, as many as I wanted.’ Her neighbour, Fred, had picked up a van load and brought them to her. They looked really good. ‘How clever of you,’ I exclaimed.

The problem manifested a couple of weeks later. The garden reeked of rotting fish and the stink pervaded the house. It gradually worsened and necessitated Mum buying a hosepipe and standing there day after day, washing the shells until eventually the smell became almost tolerable. I don’t think she went out into the yard much that summer.

Mum couldn’t tolerate waste in any form. To her mind, greed was a cardinal sin. Anything fancy, frilly or ostentatious sickened her and this translated into disparagement towards people whose desires were materially orientated and those who didn’t appreciate the natural world. ‘Look at that view,’ she'd say with a sense of wonder. 'That's completely free!' For good measure, she would usually add: 'People are so ignorant,' or something similar.

It went against the grain for her to ask for help from the State, yet I shuddered when I imagined her as she tried to cope all on her own. Going shopping in her local Co-op was enormously stressful for her, I'd discovered. Able-bodied shoppers frequently made use of the conveniently placed disabled parking bays and that made her furious. She admitted being constantly terrified of falling. Like a beetle, she had no ability to get up again because her legs had no strength.

Mum rarely left her house in those days. She had become somewhat reclusive, saying that she needed her space and loved her solitude. Every day she sat at her ancient computer, which was not connected to the internet, and wrote. She was about to have her second book published when she became unwell. Writing was her great passion, giving her joy and satisfaction. Her lonely existence was not unusual for a writer, and anyway it wasn't lonely, she assured us. Company would have felt like an intrusion. Was she brave, content and self-sufficient, or was she in denial? It was hard to know for sure. At what point should the children of elderly parents intervene and put an end to independent living?

All the rest and care Mum was receiving was making it more likely she would live into her nineties – not that she wanted to become a nonagenarian. She was making a good recovery from the severe shingles attack that had flattened her and that may have contributed to her blackout. But there was still the chronic underlying problem: the neurological condition with no name and no understandable diagnosis that prevented messages from reaching and prompting her muscles. Her right arm was also affected now. The tea in her cup rippled and swelled threateningly as she tried to keep control of its voyage through the air. She had always hated tea but now quite enjoyed what she called an 'oxymoron': a nice cup of tea. She seemed to enjoy it all: being cared for, tea, food, life. I began to imagine that one day she'd be able to use her antediluvian computer. I loved the idea that she might start writing again.

I had taken the liberty of putting Mum on a high-nutrition diet. No junk, no sweets, no coffee, refined starch or alcohol. These had been her staples, pretty much, along with the minuscule meals she used to make for herself. She'd always loved cooking but admitted that, lately, she had strayed into comfort eating. The sweets were to compensate for her loneliness which, at the time, she didn't recognise any more than my brother and I did.

Depriving her of these delights might sound heavy-handed but she said she didn't miss them. She had treats and really appreciated them, but she agreed that a simple, natural diet was a good idea and would give her a fighting chance of attaining optimum health and recovering her strength. Her mental attitude was also crucial. I encouraged her to keep mobile and as fit as was reasonable for a disabled woman of eighty-three. I couldn't have carried her, and I couldn't face having to do everything for her, had she given up and become totally incapable.

Thankfully Mum had always shunned prescribed medicines except in life-or-death circumstances, so she was not confused and suffused with a cocktail of chemicals fighting with each other as well as with her body's natural inclination to balance and heal itself. So far she had been optimistic and determined. Every day she stood and walked a few steps with her walker in front and me behind, pushing the wheelchair in case she fell backwards. We were a funny little procession. Her coughing fits had subsided, though she still had difficulty swallowing.

Mum always used to sing to herself but since her collapse she'd found even speaking uncomfortable. That didn't stop her talking, it just made her sound croaky. Now she was beginning to sound stronger and clearer again. My daughter came to look after her granny one night so that I could get out of the house. She looked puzzled as we shared a pot of tea the next day, asking, 'Why does Granny sing German opera?'

'Why indeed?' I mused. Later, I asked Mum where all this German opera came from.

'I've never sung any such thing, ever,' she said, slightly affronted.

One Monday in March a builder arrived. Roof-slates and downpipes were replaced; leaking door and window frames were repaired. The house felt increasingly watertight. I'd abandoned ship over the years, turning a blind eye to the fact that it was falling into disrepair, as I had no resources to pay for the work. When I did visit I felt mild panic and sometimes shock at its condition. Now it had to be done for Mum's sake and it was easier to do it for someone else. For her it had to be warm and dry, and black mould had to be eradicated. She insisted on paying for the repairs. The weight of worrying about the state of the house lightened.

The sky was brightening. Birds were starting to sing in the mornings – they knew that spring was waiting in the wings. The weeks rolled by and each one was marked by some small improvement – a slight decrease in pain, a minute achievement. This was good news, yet with the renewed energy came the return of aspects of Mum's personality that I thought had fallen away for good. She seemed to want to get back down to the familiar business of worrying, and of planning things that can't be planned.

Decisions needed to be made regarding Mum's empty house, and that led to thoughts about what lay ahead. I could see how this stressed her. Strangely, uncertainties and projections about the future brought the past along with them. There was a return to mulling and brooding on long-dead stories, a review of old resentments and the judgements that accompanied them. Perhaps she was un-surrendering and re-arming herself. Old habits die hard. They offer proof of who we believe ourselves to be: someone we recognise; a comfortably familiar collection of conditioned responses.

Her mind seemed to run on some sort of energy that was not apparent or available to me. Some days she would get stuck on a carousel of negative thoughts and historical gripes. This was how she had been, at times, before her collapse. She clung to her pessimism, claiming, 'This is what it's like when you're my age: you look back and you regret; you look ahead and worry. You can't help it.' I guessed that, living alone, she'd felt the present didn't offer as much interest as the past. The future might be uncertain but worrying about it was a good distraction. None of this seemed to make her happy.

I was committed to using all the energy and resources I had to help and encourage Mum in being fully alive while she was here. Whilst I wanted to honour her desire to rely on her cosy old ways, I did not want to collude with her anxiety, or her tendency to criticise others and undermine herself. It seemed a subtle and tricky challenge to support her without reinforcing what I saw as her illusions, and her mind-talk.

If possible, I would steer her gently towards the calm waters of the present. I wanted to keep things positive and, crucially, to protect the feeling of sanctuary I had created. Even though this was *my* house, my mother was still my mother and I was in danger of losing my footing and slipping into her way of interacting with the world. I was at risk of reverting to the child I had been long ago; I feared that the peace I had worked hard to secure within myself would be destroyed by her pervasive anxiety and her negativity.

There was nobody on earth I could possibly have known longer than my mother. She had known me forever, yet I had always felt she knew me less well than she thought she did. Rather than find out where I stood or what I might have to offer, she made assumptions about me and my perspectives. She was somehow bigger than me.

Mum often focussed on *the* past and *her* past. Strangely though, we never talked about *our* past or *our* relationship. She had always claimed she had completely forgotten great chunks of it but that might have been a convenient excuse. Perhaps she felt overwhelmed by the idea of unpicking and examining our tightly-packed historical baggage. It might have looked like a can of worms to her and she possibly didn't have the appetite or tools to navigate that particular shared experience. She might have thought it preferable to avoid the subject altogether, and it must have appeared to her that I felt the same way because, over the course of my life, I had lost my impetus to confront and learned how to play along.

I hoped that we were old enough and wise enough to

review events, clear up misunderstandings, and untangle knots. I hoped we could heal our relationship. Perhaps that was idealistic and maybe it was safer not to excavate our history. After all, I had tried that several times before and been met with a solid defensive wall: she had a clever way of diverting the flow of the conversation away from the subject and into a story of her own. Sometimes, she would claim she had no memory of the issue and if I pressed further she would suddenly be too tired to deal with what she felt might be viewed as my complaints about her. Mum hadn't lacked maternal instinct in general. She wasn't cold, either. It was more that my childhood and teenage problems, especially the emotional ones, had been an inconvenience. It was beyond her capacity or willingness to deal with them and so she had little appetite for revisiting them.

❧

This was not a career move. It wasn't a job with hours, and pay, or holidays. This was twenty-four hours a day on call, every day. I'd been caring for Mum for a few months when something crept out of the shadows and showed itself. I remembered receiving, back in the first few weeks, the gentle, well-meant warnings from friends – people in the know. At the time their words had floated through my brain without really taking hold; it seemed they might have been relevant to someone else, but not to me. 'You'll think you can do this forever but you can't, and you must not feel guilty when you come to realise that you just can't carry on anymore. You must plan ahead,' they'd said. I'd filed that away for some much later time but, suddenly, here it was. I knew I couldn't keep this up for the long-term.

❧

One Sunday David and I visited Mum's old house to fetch some more of her belongings. She decided not to accompany us. We left her alone, resting in bed for a few hours, and let ourselves into her little terraced house: a world where everything she had collected and created over a lifetime remained. There were the beloved paintings, family photographs, her antique dining chairs, her wedding-present cutlery, the overgrown garden with its bird bath and the wooden bench that had been her second husband's favourite seat – evidence of her past that painted a vivid picture of her personality.

I climbed the stairs, sidling past her stair lift. I saw the bath hoist that she'd used every evening. I recalled the last time I'd witnessed her trying to exit the bath, just before her collapse. I'd been shocked at the time, realising she could no longer be left to manage this risky operation alone.

As I stood in her simple kitchen, just for a moment, I felt I was my mother visiting 'my' old life. Seeing through her eyes, I imagined what it might be like for her, facing this one-way street. I could see all that she had given up. For the first time in a long time I cried. I grieved for the life that was now over, for both of us. I would never again visit her in this place; this version of her was gone.

A couple of days later Mum started behaving strangely and getting very agitated about what I thought were very small concerns in the scheme of things. It turned out that, like me, she had come to realise she was captive in a situation neither of us would have chosen. She felt guilty that I had given up so much and had to work long hours to support her. She also felt beholden to me and frustrated by her reduced independence. She felt powerless.

The small things that irritated her were merely symptoms of frustration with the fact that she could no longer do things her own way. There was a new energy emanating from her. She had insisted for example that I draw all the curtains in my entire house – not just the ones in her room – well before dusk to keep the heat in, and I had argued for enjoying the last of the scarce winter daylight, while suggesting that the double glazing would keep her warm. She was determined to have the upper hand and there was a sharp, unfriendly edge to her voice. She was speaking to me in that way that warned me not to argue. She was the boss. Why did this matter so much to her? Was it about heat conservation or something else?

It seemed that she really wanted a battle, something she'd always enjoyed. That takes two, and if I wanted peace perhaps I had to let go of my end of the stick and be prepared to lose the argument. But I felt fear rising in me. I knew something needed to be nipped in the bud, even though I was not clear what it was. Why did it matter so much to me?

I heard myself saying, 'I think we need to be careful how we talk to one another. Let's try to be kind and respectful, whatever we need to say, even if we have different opinions.' It felt strange to say that to my mother, and more like the way I could imagine talking to a child. I could have said, 'This is *my* house' but that felt too harsh. We both knew that it was my house and she was my guest. That was the issue.

Mum sat silently on her bed, giving me a look that I couldn't interpret. I closed her curtains and left. And as the evening drew in, I decided to let go of the daylight and embrace early closing as she had wanted me to. I'd made my point.

The patterns of the past were coming to life in our interactions. This was less about who won the seemingly petty battle of the curtains and more about a deeper issue that had always been present in our relationship: something I wasn't willing to allow to take root in my home. I was determined stop us straying blindly onto the beginning of a slippery decline where hostile communication become casual and normal. It was not normal, or tolerable, for me.

⁂

Spring was getting into full swing. Things were now running smoothly on a practical level and Mum and I were cordial and respectful – polite, even. However, something was brewing. One morning her face looked set and stern. She seemed troubled. 'What's up? I asked.

'I don't like the way you are; you seem... different... too nice... not like your old self,' she said.

'Charming!' I thought.

The honeymoon period was over, it seemed. The gloves were off. My mother was done with surrendering and had had enough of readying herself for death. She would not be going anywhere ethereal just yet after all. If she had regained some fighting spirit that had to be a good thing, if not an easy thing.

'You're always smiling a little too much,' she said, mimicking my smile. She had been brooding and had come to the conclusion that I was being false: putting on a cheerful expression while secretly seething with resentment towards her. Was she merely projecting onto me how she might have felt in my shoes? I'd thought I was doing well, taking pride in my new job and learning to do it with efficiency and even joy.

Perhaps she was envious, annoyed that I seemed happy while she was drifting into dissatisfaction or even despair about her reduced circumstances. Or it could have been that what she was seeing didn't match her familiar old picture of me. Had she lost a daughter over whom she had always had some sort of power and gained a carer who was able to exercise a degree of professional detachment and control over the situation?

Mothers can wound with their words, whether they intend to or not. I felt stung and wrong-footed. I knew that there was some truth in what she said. I *had* changed over the years. Was she able to see me more clearly than I could see myself? What if I *was* putting on an act, and didn't even know it? What if the optimistic attitude that I had embraced – which seemed to be bringing me relative peace and contentment – was just a lot of nonsense: straws clutched by a delusional fool on a desperate quest? Suddenly, my secure relationship with myself crumbled into a confused heap.

'Fuck you!' I shouted once I had descended the steps into the kitchen and out of earshot. I was furious with my mother for what I saw as an attempt to cut me down to size and wipe the smile off my face. I suddenly feared that I had walked right into a trap. I had no escape as my precious sanctuary was now occupied by someone I had kept at a safe distance until very recently. My autonomy was gone. That added up to two women both feeling powerless in one house.

I seethed and prepared lunch. I'd guessed that our history was lurking in some dark corner not too far away. We had both been doing a good job of keeping it there, but how long can anyone succeed at that? We'd been doing so well that I had begun to wonder if my wounds were all nicely healed after all. I didn't really know if my mother had wounds in relation to me particularly. We'd never had that conversation.

I'd let my defences down. I didn't think I'd been keeping up a façade, but if I had then it might not have been a good idea to prod at it. By the same token, I didn't want to encounter what hid in the depths of my mum's darker recesses.

From somewhere deep inside me a voice whispered, encouraging me to observe my mind with its well-trodden pathways and patterns and to avoid getting pulled down by old thinking. Hadn't I come to know myself in recent years, and finally started to feel comfortable in my own skin? Hadn't I discovered that what I am is, in fact, solid bedrock from which 'I' can never fall? Was my inner peace really so fragile? Was I an adult, a teenager or a child?

I heeded the whispering voice, and then I let go; my anger was replaced by the consoling thought that, despite what the mirror says, I am not my mother. This situation, in which I could potentially feel trapped, was surely the acid test: an opportunity to find a way to be honest, to stand up for myself, and to find the key to feeling emotionally safe around my mother.

❧

At last, I'd booked Mum into a rest home so that I could take a week off. It had sounded like a caring and pleasant place and it was. The staff were lovely smiling women who attended to all the needs of the very elderly and frail. Though I visited twice, Mum insisted that I stay away and get a proper break. 'I'm having a marvellous rest. It's so nice here,' she assured me, smiling and wafting her hand in the over-heated air of the small bland room.

I stayed with David, where I slept a great deal and had

some time to think. I thought about my mother a lot. I really did care about her, whether I wanted to or not. Along with that came a heavy sense of responsibility. I felt alone with my burden – there was nobody who could take my place, or even understand how I felt. These were rational and understandable feelings.

I was also experiencing something else that was harder to grasp or explain. It had to do with the simple fact that she and I were entangled in a lifelong, possibly karmic entwinement. This was ridiculously obvious yet the meaning of it was touching me in a new and potent way.

I had kept Mum at a distance for a lot of my adult life. To achieve that I'd had to bury a lot of things and I'd had to give up hope – the vain hope of Mum being the source of dependable support. I'd had to let things be as they were and move on. Yet there had been no escape from the deep, inherent entanglement. My mother was part of my life and she was part of me. My youthful attempt to challenge the assertion that blood is thicker than water had not altered the facts. I had wanted to wriggle out of that cliché and free myself from the role that I had inherited, and I had failed. I always had been, and always would be, my mother's daughter. This was now evident in a very literal way. It wasn't so much that I was like her as the fact that I couldn't escape her now. I couldn't abandon her.

❧

The struggle to be myself had been a quiet and private rebellion: a process happening inside my mind that I could not share. I had no words for it and nobody else would understand anyway. I thought that was obvious because everybody else seemed to be doing fine. It was my unique problem.

Mum had always seemed oblivious, probably believing that our relationship was good enough. And perhaps it was, objectively, but my experience of childhood was entirely subjective. I sometimes thought I was defective: a freak who couldn't fall in with family culture; a misfit unable to play the game with the rest of the team. Meanwhile my mother had simply gone about her business. It seemed as though she didn't notice my discomfort.

When she needed me, Mum *knew* that I would be there for her. She assumed I would slot into the role of dutiful daughter because I was her daughter. Yet I had always been wary about asking *her* for help – particularly emotional support – because in general I had received short shrift. My survival as an infant depended on her care, love, nurture and support. My security as an emerging person relied upon these same gifts that I had never assumed were mine for the taking.

Certain strategies, conscious or otherwise, had worked for Mum, just as they had for many other people. She feared being overwhelmed by her emotions so kept tight control of them, "mastered" them. She was rather lax when it came to honing empathy skills and had developed the ability to overlook certain responsibilities. She seemed not to concern herself too much with consequences, preferring to live what she would describe as 'a short life and a gay one'.

Perhaps that fit neatly with the belief she had held for decades that God was about to call her at any moment, and her more recent worry that on Judgement Day, He might take a dim view and send her to "the wrong place". She'd had her fun, leapt onto the merry-go-round of life, throwing caution to the wind, and danced into the arms of men she couldn't resist – didn't want to resist. She'd grabbed the best out of life and who could blame her?

Expressing my feelings and needs might have exposed what she disliked about women and shone a light onto something she kept hidden and repressed in herself: her vulnerability. I knew not to do that. It was too risky for me.

❧

Over the decades, Mum had told me stories about her childhood years. She was seven years old when the Second World War broke out. Like all her friends, she carried a gas mask everywhere which made her feel fearful, she said, but it was the horrible siren that terrified her each and every time it went off. 'But we never grumbled in those years,' she told me. 'If anyone moaned about anything they were brought up sharp. It was "Don't you know there's a war on?" It just wasn't done to complain.'

She lived in relatively safe Yorkshire and her mother's crafty kitchen skills meant there was just about enough to eat. It was a good time, she assured me. It was her parents' generation who had been traumatised. The Great War had already broken them. It was hard to imagine what effect that catastrophe had had on them as citizens and as parents.

My maternal grandmother was a placid, dependable woman who tended to take the line of least resistance. Mum was slightly disparaging about my gran's quiet acceptance and had felt frustrated in her youth by what she saw as a lack of spark. However, Mum's eyes filled with sorrow when she told me that Gran never, ever spoke about her Great War. Gran was nineteen when she received the news that her fiancé had been killed in action. Much later Gran met and married my grandfather and devoted herself to him and her new family as it grew.

My gran was not given to emotional incontinence. She was the embodiment of stability and a safe haven for me. I could depend on her, predict her behaviour and understand her rules, which were few but unchangeable. She also had a softness and sensitivity which I perceived intuitively and respected profoundly.

By being consistent my gran allowed me to know her and know where I stood in relation to her. The simplicity of her life made her available: she was always present and had time for me. She was always there and I always knew she loved me. As far as I could tell, she was never dishonest, possibly because dishonesty was not in her emotional vocabulary and also because secrecy wasn't needed. She had nothing to hide. It came naturally to me to avoid doing anything that would hurt or offend her because I knew her well and loved her more than I loved anyone.

Mum described her parents as Victorian, which was a historical fact rather than a criticism. Her upbringing had been orderly yet wonderfully happy, she said. She idolised her father who she considered to be 'ahead of his time', in part because he believed strongly in the power of education for both boys and girls.

He nurtured Mum's intellect and she was a devoted and able scholar of English. She was also a tree-climbing tomboy, headstrong and mad about horses. Her father might have hoped that she would go to university and have a brilliant career, possibly in journalism, but she chose to work outdoors teaching horse-riding. She had found a life that she truly loved but it wasn't long before she got distracted. My dashing father caught her eye and within a few years they were engaged.

While my parents were planning their wedding, tragedy struck: Mum's only sibling, her beloved brother, died of heart failure aged twenty-nine, leaving his widow to bring up their baby boy alone. Not long after the tragedy my maternal grandfather died "of a broken heart". Mum had always appeared brave – perhaps too brave – about this devastating double loss. I could not know exactly how this had affected her. Her long-absorbed grief was intangible to me yet I always felt deep sadness for Mum, Gran, my widowed auntie and her fatherless infant son.

Years later, when Mum had two boys of her own, she named her second son after her late brother. Shockingly he, my brother, contracted leukaemia and died when he was thirty-seven. That loss we shared. Again, she was brave and stoical, to the point that her best friend worried that she was in complete denial. But I knew her by then and I recognised something in her. She was abnormally calm, and she was wistful but not miserable – she never fell apart. She was made of something incredibly resilient. Perhaps that was in her nature or maybe she was just accustomed to loss.

I had never thought of myself as resilient. Still, after my brother died, I discovered capacities that I hadn't known I possessed. Mum noticed this. She marvelled at it and leaned in towards me. She sensed my strength and was grateful for my support. For a time, I found myself in a new position: standing shoulder to shoulder with my mum. We had not resolved the past but it seemed irrelevant in contrast to the tragedy that had brought us abruptly into a new present. We became closer and our relationship enjoyed a new phase based on improved mutual respect and appreciation. At first it was intense but gradually, over the months, the elastic between us loosened again. We both got on with our lives and kept in warm, regular, though not overly frequent, contact.

❧

All too soon it was time to collect Mum and take her home. She seemed quiet, resigned and sad. Once we were in the car I asked, 'How was it *really*, Mum?'

'Well, it's a very caring place. There were lots of lovely helpers and the inmates seemed happy.'

'But?' I prompted, as we negotiated the lunchtime traffic.

'Well... Oh dear, I'm being critical, I know.'

'It's okay, go on...'

'Well... I felt like I'd handed my soul in at the door. I wasn't sure I'd get it back.'

'What on earth do you mean?'

'Those mountains of mashed potato...' She drifted off, looking out of the passenger window.

'Mum, is this a metaphor? I asked, wondering if she had ever seen the film *Close Encounters of the Third Kind* – the scene where the dad gets a message about a mountain via a plate of mashed spuds.

'No, it was just insipid, watery mash. It haunts me,' she sighed dramatically.

'Was there any other food?' I asked, concentrating hard on the road, and feeling alarmed.

'Oh yes, of course, and plenty of it.'

'Oh. That's good then. So, it was just a problem with the mash?'

'Yes... really, though, it was the sapping of my will. Halfway through the week I was ready to give in and let myself just...' She trailed off.

'What?' I pressed.

'Well, the other people were all so much closer than me.'

'Closer? Did you feel left out?' I asked.

'No, no. I realised, you know... I realised I am not quite as close as I thought.'

'Close? Close to what? ... Ah I see. You were the most alive and able one there?' I laughed.

'Mmm. And I feel horribly ungrateful but, I don't do well with... institutions, rules. And, do you know? It was lonelier there, surrounded by people, than in my little kennel in your house with all its clutter and things.'

'Yeah, I know. I'm sorry if it was torture for you.'

'It wasn't that bad at all, it's just that if I'd stayed any longer I'd have lost my will to live.'

I drove up the hill to my village feeling sad and a bit guilty.

'I'm sorry, Mum. Thanks for giving me a week off.'

'Don't mention it. It was my pleasure... Well, you know what I mean.'

'I do, and you know, Mum, it has shown you something.'

'Has it? What?'

'You still have a life to live, something to strive for.'

We were comfortably silent for the rest of the journey. Mum was hugely relieved to get back to her room. The break had done us both good and Mum seemed positive and appreciative. The days were getting longer and the workload felt more manageable after my rest. I had it all running like a well-oiled machine.

❧

What is a reasonable amount of time to spend on Scrabble? Is it one of those things where moderation is important? Can one have an unhealthy relationship with the game – even an addiction? When Mum first arrived in my house it seemed unlikely we would ever play it again. And then one day I came in to find her puzzling over a cryptic crossword and we started doing the odd clue together. Things improved further. We talked about playing Scrabble and her face lit up at the idea. Before long we were playing every afternoon. We were well matched, both in our standard and in our love of the game. Soon Mum was back in the saddle. Then she started winning. We would settle down with tea and home-made flapjacks and drift off into a world of words. It felt like safe territory.

One Saturday morning David was asleep in my bed. I was dozing, emerging from a dream. 'Is today special?' I asked him drowsily. What I'd had in mind was to find out if there was something we were supposed to be doing, going to the tip for example. He answered sleepily, 'Every day is special.' I felt myself smiling. I'd been seeing myself in my mind's eye: my tiny, short life as a minute dot in a vast universe. I was high up and far away. I could see life as a happening, a fleeting thing like a shooting star.

The preciousness of my time here on earth was obvious to me during those days. The sense of time racing – life passing me by – felt like a massive pressure.

It had been several months since Mum had come, via A&E, to live in my house. Having assumed she was about to die, she was doing extremely well. Thanks to the excellent work of the physiotherapist who visited twice every week, she started regaining core strength, flexibility and confidence. She looked much better and seemed happier. Now, instead of slopping around in the dressing gown of doom, she dressed herself every morning, even though that involved a lot of exertion. She had shaken off her shroud and come out of her cave to join in with life. She smiled and laughed more. She wouldn't let me do anything for her that she could do for herself. I would stand back, just being there in case she got stuck while she stretched and reached. We continued playing Scrabble every day.

The weather was on our side at last and we seemed to be settled in a harmonious phase. Our relationship felt lighter. I was enjoying being around her more than I had in times gone by, but then for no reason that I could understand, Mum snapped back into the old pattern: brooding, criticism, grudges and anxiety. Perhaps there was a well of sadness inside her that needed to express itself and I wondered if it had been a great effort for her to stay positive. Something must have triggered this sudden change. Maybe, lulled into a sense of relaxation, she had taken her eye off the ball.

Now she was trapped in a familiar but vicious cycle where the more she focussed on negative judgements and fearful thoughts, the more they grew and seemed real, giving her mind something to chew on and convincing her she had something to worry and complain about. She seemed caught in a drama that looked unreal to me. Her thoughts and feelings came like a whirlwind, scooping her up and dumping her down in a heap.

Feeling exasperated one afternoon, I implored her to stop complaining and criticising, and focus on more enjoyable topics. She replied passionately, with a touch of indignation and a mouth full of flapjack: 'I *like* complaining. I *enjoy* having a good moan.' Oats were flying into the air and I suddenly realised I was living with someone who positively revelled in the negativity that I was trying to steer her away from. I had to laugh.

I was a bit frightened of my mum during my childhood, a period which, in relation to my mother, was still ongoing to some extent. I was unsure where I stood because sometimes we had a laugh together but not always. She was unpredictable. She had a habit of saying things like, 'Well, obviously, anyone in their right mind would think…' or 'You'd have to be absolutely stupid or mad to disagree with me on this.' This was accompanied by a withering look that seemed to bore into my soul. Her tone of voice implied great authority. I had hated that when I was younger. It was hard to find my own voice and difficult to know who I was and what I thought.

But now I was beginning to see this as quite amusing. Hers were not genuine questions, but comments, gauntlets thrown down that didn't require agreement, or even a reply. I had taken her too seriously all along and, actually, I needed to lighten up and let it all go.

The past no longer mattered and it didn't impact on the present "me". Yet I could see that something had crushed my confidence as a child and caused me to become defensive, even hostile, around my mother. Revisiting the story of my life felt like reading between the lines. A pattern had been knitted into my personality and into the fabric of our relationship. We couldn't unpick all those stitches. We had to work with the material we had.

Being around Mum all day, every day, I had the opportunity to watch turbulent weather systems come and go in someone I knew very well and whom I loved unconditionally, even when I didn't like her very much. Perhaps I could view it as a free learning tool, a mirror for seeing inside my own mind's patterns. Perhaps I could just ignore it. If only I could unhook myself, stand back a little – not take it personally.

Mum wrote fiction. Her first published work was a murder mystery and I suspect she admired dark complex characters: their clever competitiveness; their ability to put someone down neatly and effectively; their tendency to win battles and arguments and to get away with misdemeanours – even homicide. She prided herself on being crafty and a little devious when deviousness was called for. She even boasted about her excellent "poker face". It must have been good because I didn't think I'd ever noticed it.

It struck me as strange that she exposed these secrets, showing me the cards she could have kept up her sleeve. In venting her nastier thoughts and judgements she was allowing her dark inner workings to be seen; perhaps there was a sweet innocence in that, or supreme self-confidence: she trusted that I would love her anyway.

Spring was bursting with promise, blossom, birdsong and sunlight. I had nobody telling me how difficult the job was and I reconnected with the way I had felt right at the beginning of the year. It was as though I was doing exactly what life required of me and not thinking too much about it, not planning, projecting, worrying or longing for it to be different. I threw myself into my daily tasks with renewed enthusiasm and a sense of fun. My work really felt like love in action. Scrabble helped.

My brother was taking care of the disposal of Mum's old house, arranging for it to go back to the trust that owned it and taking it off Mum's shoulders. He did what he could from a distance. He often thanked me for what I was doing in relation to our mother and praised my hard work, which was good to hear. He felt guilty that it was impossible for him to help with the day-to-day care.

We had always been extremely close considering our seven-year age difference and the fact that we seemed to come from entirely different planets. If I said that to him – the bit about coming from different planets – it would make him crazy. I like to keep an open mind on the origin of the species – he's a scientist. He believes that things that can't be measured and proved are likely to be twaddle. He doesn't want to persecute anyone over it – he's a really nice guy – he just has no time for nonsense; no tolerance for people who *believe* in stuff.

I suspected he thought that our mother was a bit of a "god-botherer" – and therefore wrong-headed – because she had some sort of faith in some unseen support that she perceived as helpful to her in some sort of way, a bit like an invisible bra. She bothered no-one with this, held no placard, and bore no ill will towards anyone else's beliefs. Though she did take the liberty of winding up her son with a 'God bless' at the end of letters and visits which annoyed him and made her laugh.

I fixed up a tiny kitchen area in Mum's room with a kettle, toaster and mini fridge. She was delighted to be able to make her own breakfast and brew coffee. She said, 'Maybe I could have my own little place again one day, with a bit of support.' This was a good thing to have as a goal. 'It's early days,' I said, 'but if you keep improving like this maybe you could do it.' I did some research into sheltered accommodation.

May was hot and sunny. The whole garden was bursting with life and weeds. The house, which had been in a state that could have been described as "shabby chic" (though "chic" might have been stretching the truth) had been repainted and all the windows renovated. Just looking at it from the garden gave me joy.

However, I soon hit another wall of exhaustion. It was an effort to keep going. I could never fully relax. I had very little time simply to be – to gather my wits or to do nothing at all, if the fancy took me.

The situation could not go on indefinitely. What had started out as a response to a crisis had normalised into something else: it had become my whole life and I was acutely aware that it was ticking away. Nobody was about to come to my rescue. It was up to me to direct things and not to allow myself to become the only person Mum depended on. I couldn't be all things to her. I cared for her needs and I was there for a chat, but I couldn't be her only and constant companion. I felt alone.

I knew Mum wanted more autonomy and I recognised that she'd had to give up a lot. Really, despite having excelled at living an isolated, unsociable life, she was lonely. She needed friends of her own, but she wasn't likely to make any at my house and had no interest in going anywhere where she might meet people.

I felt for her and didn't know how to help her. I couldn't just dump her in a place she didn't like, with other elderly folks, and I didn't want her to feel rejected. But at some point I'd have to live my life. I was concerned that the longer the situation went on the more difficult it would be to change things.

❦

It was June and Mum had reached a plateau: She was free of acute pain and, though weak, she was no longer exhausted, but her mobility and dexterity were unlikely to improve. I couldn't visualise a set-up that would be just right for her level of ability; where she could live semi-independently. She didn't need a nursing home but I wasn't sure if she would ever be ready for the level of independence she'd need to manage the little place of her own that she dreamed of. If she tried it and failed, that could knock her confidence back down and leave her feeling depressed and hopeless. Then her options would be severely reduced.

Timing was important. Mum needed to keep on walking steadily forward, honing skills and building up her confidence. We both needed to be patient. We were doing all right, especially in contrast to people with more significant problems. It was no use my trying to fix something that wasn't ready to be fixed – that only made my brain spin. I decided to enjoy the summer without worrying too much about our longer-term futures. I called off the search, postponing it until autumn. A solution would show itself, I was sure.

❦

It was August. I had been sharing my house with my mother for eight months. Sitting outside in the sunshine each afternoon had relaxed her and lifted her spirits. Her sunny mood seemed to be holding. Mum relished her time in the garden and she loved my house. 'It's a spiritual house. It's got good vibes,' she told me.

She said my care of her had made her well and that she

was truly happy even though it had been a wrench for her to let go of her independence. She would say, 'Thank you for being so patient with me – I don't know how you do it.' I didn't know how I did it either. It was a complete mystery.

I was enjoying my house too and making the best of things. But I had left the life I had chosen – a life I loved. That was a challenge for both David and me. Our time together had become fragmented, our plans abandoned. Our future was uncertain. I feared that our paths might diverge further and, through no fault of either of us, we might find ourselves on separate tracks looking back on a strong relationship and the happy times we'd once had, rueing the day we had stopped seeing the bigger picture and let something good get destroyed because we couldn't work out a way to meet the needs of all concerned. Sometimes I felt that I was losing him. I was too tired to feel miserable; I was simply numb.

David continued with his life and work in Pembrokeshire. We talked on the phone most evenings and one night he announced that he was going to be a grandfather the following year. I was delighted, yet I suddenly felt as though I was witnessing the life of people I cared about from another planet. I had become a ghost in my old life which seemed to be continuing quite well without me. I needed to hear something that would reassure me that I still mattered or even existed.

In September Mum was very excited when some good friends offered us the chance to house-sit their beautiful home close to David's place. We installed ourselves and settled in for a three-week holiday.

David and I were able to live together while Mum had the granny flat and access to the magnificent garden which delighted her. It was idyllic. My brother and his family stayed for a few days while David and I went off to The Yorkshire Dales for the wedding of a close friend of mine.

When we got back to our holiday abode, Mum reminded me that we had talked about the sheltered housing complex that had recently been completed in a nearby town. She was curious to see what it was like, fantasising that one day she might be ready to consider living in such a place. Now, I realised, the time for procrastination was over.

We drove along the country lanes to a really attractive modern building with pretty gardens. Everything was geared up for people with disabilities. We bumped into the manager who offered to show us one of the flats. I wheeled Mum in and, straight ahead, through the large windows, she was faced with the view.

'Look at the magnificent mountain!' Mum was enchanted. 'Look at the kitchen and the walk-in shower!'

'This is the last empty flat,' said the manager. 'So if you want it you'd better tell me now.'

'I want it,' announced my mother, who was grinning and staring out of the window. I followed her gaze towards the beautiful mountain and remembered the conversation about the mashed potato when I'd collected her from the rest home. Had she received some sort of prophetic message back then?

❧

I was sitting at my desk for a snatched moment, looking out across the rooftops to the flat river valley and the woods beyond. In May I'd watched as it transformed from bare to fully clothed in bright greens, and now I was witnessing winter being born again. A steady breeze stripped the colour away in a continuous eastward stream of leaves. The trees were getting naked just when they needed an extra layer. They looked cold and thin. Just beyond my window the last apples fell, and on a spindly branch sat a robin.

I had accepted the season, finally surrendering after a futile tussle, during which I felt a massive 'NO!' groan through my being: a seemingly endless moment that started at the end of September when, one day, there had been an emphatic nip heralding the sudden death of the summer. The nights drew in fast and forced the shutting of curtains, some of which had remained open, without interruption or comment, for months.

Over the summer I'd trusted that things would work out, and I sometimes worried that my faith was misplaced: that I was merely indulging in avoidance and procrastination. But sure enough, in late September, Mum had found her flat and had been accepted as a supported independent resident.

In a few months she would move and I'd be footloose. I'd also be free of guilt because I had not pushed Mum – she had decided to jump, taking a leap of faith in herself. I was grateful for that and I admired her pluck. Now, because she knew she would have to, she summoned up all her strength. Now, because I knew it wouldn't go on forever, I could enjoy my job wholeheartedly.

It felt as though magic had happened. For me there could not have been a better solution than the one that presented itself on the last day of our holiday, when we'd visited the sheltered housing complex. Mum, however, was feeling apprehensive about what she had decided to do. She was taking a risk and she wondered how she would cope alone in a new environment. She had several weeks to gather her wits and prepare herself for the move. Practically, all she'd have to do was allow me to pack up her things and drive her to her new home. But psychologically she had to climb Everest. She didn't feel ready. It would be an upheaval – so many new things to learn.

⁂

Each day the pale sun hung level with my window. I started to view the approaching winter with optimism. There was light at the end of the tunnel and it looked inviting and comforting. However, I had become conditioned to my reduced-sized world and feared that when Mum moved out I might feel disorientated. How would I know what to do? Would I miss playing Scrabble? Would I miss her?

A couple of hours each afternoon spent making words fit together on a board had helped us both survive our challenging year and prevented our brain cells from dying off. It stuck me that this was how my mother and I interacted playfully, and though it was cerebral and required quiet and stillness, it was fun. The aim was to get a massive score, but the real purpose was enjoyment in the game and in each other's company.

I couldn't remember my mum playing with me when I was a child and I suspect she was a little remote; not unemotional, but distracted by things that left her with limited capacity for frivolities like horsing around with youngsters. She would intervene in the boisterous games my brother and I played, worried that we might get out of control. 'It will end in tears,' she'd say.

One day it occurred to me that, having lost her brother,

she might have found it painful to hear the hysterical laughter of over-excited siblings playing together. I put this to her as gently as I could. 'No, it was nothing like that,' she said with a laugh. 'It was just so bloody noisy.'

In December my mother moved to her flat, which was not far from where David and I had been living before the events of last Christmas altered the course of our lives. It was an upheaval and it took a huge amount of effort but, finally, there she was with her treasured furniture, the lovely view and caring staff who were on hand to help her get to grips with the new surroundings and routines.

We had been through a lot together. Mum's journey had taken her from death's door to independence. My journey seemed to have gone in exactly the opposite direction. The situation ended in the nick of time. If I'd had to stay living another year with Mum I would have withered. Something might have died.

I settled her in, went home and crashed out for a few days, feeling that I would never regain my life-force or my joy. I wailed to David, 'What on earth has it all been for? I have given everything to my mother and left myself with nothing.'

He said, 'You've done a wonderful thing. You helped your mother to get well, stand on her own feet and manage her life. Now she's able to live a life of dignity and happiness that will leave you free to enjoy your life again. Yes, it was worth it.'

Without his support, and the help of my children, I could not have moved her and her worldly goods twice and turned my house into a care home and healing sanctuary. When I imagined myself in Mum's position I knew that being loved and cared for by my son or daughter would be a priceless gift. If I could give that gift, I guessed I had to be prepared to receive it too, if I was fortunate enough to be offered it at some future time. I doubted it would be easy to accept such an offer.

❦

It was two weeks before Christmas. I had done nothing in preparation for the festivities. Normally, I would have made a Christmas pudding using my granny's recipe, put up my ancient fairy lights to cheer us up on the long dreary evenings, and maybe thought about presents: whether to buy any at all, or suggest we do Secret Santa or something minimal like that. The truth was, I had become so befuddled that I didn't care; I couldn't care. I didn't want to tempt fate with any sunny optimism about having a pleasant festive season. Instead I kept to myself a meagre shred of faith that at least I would not be visiting A&E, chasing up out-of-hours medics or spending a week alone in my mother's sitting room while she slept upstairs.

A local friend was holding a small ceremony on Christmas Eve where neighbours were invited to light a candle and express their love and thanks for anything in life that had touched them over the year. There was a sea of flames burning brightly, creating a golden glow. Right at the end, when everyone was about to get up and leave, David lit a candle and, looking at me, said, 'I hadn't appreciated how hard this year was for you. I'm sorry I didn't always understand what you were going through. You've done something challenging and amazing, and you've done it well. Thank you for being you.'

I was moved to tears and thought this was a very generous sentiment seeing as David had also made sacrifices and given so much. It hadn't been easy for him. And on occasion it was clear that his patience had worn thin, but he had been all I could have hoped for in a partner. His words meant a lot to me.

My brother and his partner joined David and me for dinner in Mum's new home where she was just beginning to find her feet, and from which she didn't want to move. She was on good form and tentatively optimistic. She had finally allowed my brother to get her a new laptop and connect it to the internet. With her familiar treasures around her, she looked very much at home.

On New Year's Eve David and I went to a party. I got chatting with a woman and told her of my year immersed in caring for Mum. I asked her about her life. She had a severely disabled daughter who she'd cared for every day for two decades. I felt humble and rather feeble when I thought about her life, and the millions of people who did so much more than I did, for much longer and in far worse circumstances than mine. I knew that they didn't always get the support and respite they needed and I knew that most of them didn't ever sign up for the role. I was in awe of these carers and felt a bit guilty for having found it so heavy at times. I reminded myself that we all have different capacities and different stories.

Something on the radio had caught my attention some time after Mum had moved in. A middle-aged man had found himself caring full-time for his aged mother who was frail and incapacitated. He described his experience as not only his duty but his privilege. That sounded noble, but I'd only caught a fragment of the programme and wondered what other contributors had shared. Had anyone found it challenging? Had someone dared, or been allowed, to say, 'I resent giving up my life to become parent to my parent, who, by the way, drives me up the wall'?

I had done my bit – done my best – and with good heart. If I had been able to predict that the end point would come when it did, I might not have felt so overwhelmed and trapped. Something happened to me over the months, though, that made it difficult for me to integrate my own life with the all-encompassing business of focussing intensely on the full-time care of another person. I lost my sense of perspective. It was all or nothing. I couldn't say why. I could only count my blessings.

Reflecting on the year that had just ended, I remembered playing Scrabble day after day in the quiet sitting room next to a roaring fire, or in the garden, under the cherry tree, listening to the birds. Quite early on, Mum had said, 'Whatever happens, if I die soon, I want you to know you have given me a gift more precious than you will ever know. I can't ever thank you adequately. You saved me.'

Part Two

Several weeks after Mum moved into her new home I was still concerned that the year of total immersion in her life had changed me permanently. I thought that I would never return to myself or retrieve any sense of direction. I was numb. I drew an imaginary line, trusting that as the year moved on, so would I. It was time to make a fresh start: to rekindle a fire that had been left unattended and inadequately fed. I had to heal my body, I felt sick and toxic. Sure enough, at some point in the New Year there was a shift: new energy came in. I found myself feeling almost excited; I was free to do anything now. From this perspective my year under house arrest had shrunk into a short story.

My life fell into a new rhythm. I had intended to move back in with David but, instead, I found myself still living in my house during the week and spending weekends with him. On the journeys between our homes I stopped in at Mum's and helped her out for a few hours twice a week. This left me with two or three days home alone each week. On these days I stayed quiet. I deep-cleaned and reorganised my house and as I did so I felt my inner wiring begin to join up correctly. I had been hungry for retreat and I cherished this precious time spent in silent solitude. I found it addictive. The new living arrangement suited David too. He had got used to having space for himself.

Mum was settling into her new life and managing very well considering she had been convinced that she was about to die, and to tell the truth, had been quite looking forward to it.

Weeks rolled on and I was doing fine. My afternoons with Mum were enjoyable. But one day she seemed glum and her face looked tense. 'I have a problem,' she announced. Apparently God had not made the journey with her to her new flat. He had been there in my house, she said, but was nowhere to be found in her new residence. Evidently it had taken her several weeks to come to this realisation. If we were going to have a conversation on this subject, I thought we had better define terms. 'What do you actually mean by "God"?' I asked.

'Well, you know... a sort of presence, a feeling; a voice inside us helping us to do better,' she said. 'He's always been there, even when I told him to go away and stopped going to church in my forties.'

'Why did you do that?' I asked.

'I didn't *want* to be good. I didn't want to be a better person. I wanted to rebel.'

Mum had lost her faith and 'gone to the bad', as she'd put it. Then, at around sixty, possibly as a result of losing her son, she had reconnected with her source of inner guidance and comfort. She had even started going to church again until quite recently when her legs got too feeble to make the weekly journey.

Our views on religion were different, but I'd always noticed that her faith, though sporadic, made her happier, kinder and sweeter. The church had kept her orientated. She'd had a path to follow and now, without it, she felt lost.

'Do you miss church?' I asked.

'Sort of. Now I have to do it all for myself, no support, no reminders. But anyway, the church has lost touch with the essence... the direct experience of...' She trailed off and then rather shakily started singing an eighth-century hymn from the Celtic church. 'Be though my vision... Thou in the darkness, still my true light...' While she was singing she looked soft and peaceful, just as she had when she'd first come to my house and surrendered her will.

She'd sung all she could remember of the hymn and said, 'I suppose I should pray more but I can't. You see, this is not a spiritual place. I know I shouldn't be thinking about how other people see me, but I do. When I go to the dining room every lunch-time I feel...'

'Vulnerable?' I prompted.

'Mmmm,' she sighed.

'I guess it's a bit of a goldfish bowl here, among the other residents. But what about God? Is He really located in a particular place, or is He inside your heart?' I asked.

'Good question,' she said. 'I know we are all part of God, but I can't *feel* it anymore.'

I wondered why God hadn't moved here with her and whispered when she needed a helping hand. Was He hiding? Perhaps He was there – and always had been – but while she thought about herself and worried about how she looked to the eyes of these strangers, her mind was too noisy to hear Him.

It was getting time for me to leave, so I simply suggested that God is everywhere, and that praying for renewed faith and connection might help. I drove away feeling glad that we'd had such a meaningful exchange, but also troubled that she felt so bereft. She'd looked so sad. It seemed that during her relatively blissful, carefree year in my house, her mind had let go of her for a while. But it had been in danger of losing a disciple and now it had come back with a vengeance to reclaim and taunt her.

Mum longed for connection, happiness and inner harmony. Talking to God seemed to help a lot with that. It always had. Going to church had given her a place to reconnect but it had also confused her and undermined her wavering faith, not in God but in her own spirituality, *her* way of bringing solace into her life.

I really hoped Mum could find peace in herself even at this late stage in her life – particularly at this late stage. I just wanted her to be happy. That was a lot to ask. I scuttled back to my tidy, quiet house for another dose of calm and solitude, and wondered if God was at home.

❧

At lunchtime every day, Mum had been sitting by herself in the dining hall, possibly feeling lonely in a crowd. Sometimes I joined her for a snack and one day I noticed a rather handsome man sitting at a nearby table. He was also dining alone and I thought, 'Wouldn't it be nice if the two of them sat together and kept each other company?' He'd looked decidedly unhappy sitting alone but when I caught his eye and greeted him, his face broke into an enormous, glassy-eyed smile.

I wasn't sure how it happened but, before long, this man, Gerald, and my mum became dining buddies. This was very fortuitous because she was not showing any signs of joining in with the other people at her new place, who lived in their independent flats like hers. Most had formed cosy groups and sat together eating and chatting. Now she had a friend of her own. I decided it was time I stopped joining her at lunchtimes, but I continued to visit frequently, delivering shopping, cleaning and doing admin and laundry. Sometimes we played

Scrabble and, always, we talked. As the weeks went by she talked more and more about Gerald.

One day I popped in on Mum and she was excited. She looked suddenly younger and I thought I saw a glint in her eye. I wondered what was making her feel so elated. Had God found her new address at last? It turned out that she and Gerald were getting on famously and that their lunchtime conversations had been stretching into the afternoons. From the way she was talking it was obvious she was keen on him and I asked her what she thought he felt about her. 'It's curious,' she told me. 'He is very attentive and always makes a beeline for me. He wants to do things for me; help me with every little thing. But I'm worried about what people will think. What if they think we're having a romance?'

'What if they do? Does it matter?' I asked.

'I'd be horrified, and anyway it's ridiculous. I'm old enough to be his mother for goodness sake. What on earth can he be getting out of this?'

'Companionship? Someone bright and witty to talk with? Who cares what people think? It's wonderful that you have a friend. Just enjoy it.'

'Hmmm, suppose you're right,' she concluded. It was lovely to see Mum happy. She seemed to be stretching herself, making an effort, partly for Gerald's benefit. Life had given Mum an unexpected gift. Maybe she'd started praying again. What exactly had she asked for?

❦

Mum had exhausted herself with her excitement over her new life and, particularly, Gerald. Now, not only did they sit together over extended lunchtimes, but they met for an evening drink too. She'd lost weight and she told me she wasn't sleeping well. There was a touch of melodrama creeping into her speech and her moods swung between agitation, romantic optimism, and pessimism. She was confused and forgetful. Perhaps her mind was suffering some normal age-related degeneration. That was to be expected, I guessed, but the decline seemed rather sudden.

She had reinstated her old habit of drinking a glass or two of wine every day, and biscuits and sweets were back on her menu, which was, of course, entirely her prerogative – there might have been very little I could do to help her maintain optimum health or to preserve her faculties. Mum had got her life back and she could choose to live it as she wished. But I now had the job of gently showing her that I had to get on with my life too. We had to let go of one another.

Mum was now thoroughly settled in her new home and had started asserting her independence. She was developing an increasingly tough stance, which seemed like great progress. If she was pulling away from me and letting go of my hand that meant she felt strong and capable, but I found that she tended to be rather more dogmatic and haughty than was necessary. She seemed combative, critical, as though she had found some old armour that she'd put away in the back of the wardrobe for a while. She no longer wanted to play Scrabble.

It was hard to understand why her attitude towards me had changed. I could see it was time for me to take my hands off the steering wheel and let her drive, so to speak. At the same time though, she still relied on me heavily – perhaps more than she realised – not only for practical things, which I was happy to do, but also, increasingly, for emotional support. I felt I was being pushed away when it came to making decisions and then pulled in when she suffered the consequences of those decisions. I was at the mercy of her drama.

The next few times I visited Mum she talked incessantly about Gerald, who was clearly very attached to her and also seemed to have a lot of influence over her. Though he was not in good health, he was a lot younger and far more energetic than she was. I couldn't help but agree with my mum that it seemed very odd that a man like Gerald would become so suddenly and intensely entwined with an elderly lady. However, she seemed more than willing to leap into the relationship. Gerald had come along and paid her a lot of attention. That must have been flattering and it might even have seemed like a last chance to fulfil a romantic fantasy.

While it seemed ideal that she had someone to share her time with, she talked as though she had suffered a traumatic emotional onslaught. She was a nervous wreck, chewing her lip as she sighed and tried, but failed, to settle in her seat. Beneath her furrowed brow her eyes looked pained and tired. I was finding it mildly alarming to listen to what sounded like the angst of a teenager with a heavy crush.

One day I asked her, 'Are you having secret meetings behind the mobility-scooter shed?'

'It's not like that. But that's quite funny actually,' she said, and she managed a laugh. That was it! I hadn't seen her laugh for ages. Humour had always been one of her strong suits, even if it was of the dry and somewhat sardonic variety. These days we rarely shared a joke. Mirth had been hijacked by angst.

Perhaps what Mum really needed was a close female friend to have fun with – someone to confide in – but she had neglected the search for a bosom pal in favour of something romantic and all-consuming, though not in any physical sense. It was extraordinary to witness this, and a bit of a shock. I was not sure I could deal with my mother's enormous feelings.

❧

Relationships between mothers and daughters are typically intense, complex and riddled with vulnerability. How can they not be, considering that we all once inhabited our mother's inner space? At sixteen, I'd thought I had broken free of my mother's apron strings when I left home, like bullet out of gun. I believed I had made a clean break that would heal and fade into an almost invisible scar. I tried to ignore my wounds. Perhaps I had only managed to absent myself physically while continuing to carry my mother around with me. Something invisible and intangible stretched between us and it was impossible to cut myself free.

During our year together there were times when I felt that Mum and I had achieved the creation of a wholesome, affectionate alliance. Our situation had the potential to bring up some tricky old stuff, and it did, but at the time the content seemed superficial. Perhaps we'd been wise to leave the depths unexplored. We got along well most of the time. I knew Mum needed me and she genuinely appreciated my devotion and support. I appreciated her generosity in sharing the household expenses.

There comes a time when it feels inappropriate and stifling for others to know what is best for us, even if they might be right. We need to mess things up for ourselves if we want to complete the rite of passage into full adulthood.

I had created a harbour for my mum, and when she regained strength and wanted to be more independent I did my best to support her. At times she was genuinely terrified and wanted to hold onto me. I had to judge when and how to leave her to fend for herself in carefully considered stages. I watched her free herself and sail away from me. This had to be a good thing.

Mum was fortunate, relatively, but increasingly she appeared disgruntled. Having launched herself headlong into an emotional storm she found herself floundering in a sea of overwhelming feelings that she was too old and too weak to cope with. She was beside herself and looked bewildered whenever I saw her. One day she finally confessed with a heavy sigh: 'I'm really quite mad at the moment.' I felt for her and I didn't know what to do.

It was difficult to know what was really going on. Mum was intensely attached to Gerald. He wanted to do everything for her, she said, but he seemed overbearing and controlling. He had even started bossing me about via her. He had taken to using Mum's email account to send me instructions about things he thought I should do – things I wasn't sure Mum had any knowledge about. He took up a lot of her time, staying late into the evenings and leaving her feeling overwhelmed and completely exhausted. She was totally open about the fact that he was bossy and opinionated and that she couldn't stand up for herself. I found this alarming, but she just sighed, saying, 'I am under Gerald's spell and I am helpless.' She spoke as though this was something wonderful, romantic and desirable.

Though Mum clearly felt incapable of standing her ground

with Gerald she was able to assert herself with me. She made it very clear that she had chosen to befriend Gerald and she had taken him into her heart; she preferred her life with Gerald in it, whatever the cost. I had been put in my place firmly and I felt confused.

Was Mum in a vulnerable position and in danger of being worn down and exploited, or was I being ridiculous and over-protective? Gerald had seemed charming when I had met him briefly, though I had barely seen him since. I wondered if he was avoiding me. I knew I had to let my mum live her life even if that meant that she got herself into trouble. But what did she expect of me now? Did she assume that after all we'd been through, we would simply fall back into our traditional roles and that she would have my daughterly obedience as well as my help? Was I willing to disappoint her? And anyway, was I really helping her if I stood by and watched her lose her sanity without at least saying something?

As I was mowing the lawn one afternoon a phrase popped into my head: *Love is not a pie*. Along with the phrase a memory was emerging clearly. As I was growing up, whenever my mum became enamoured of a new male companion, she changed completely. Typically, her attention would drift off into some lofty place that I couldn't see, and she would float away, high above all earthly concerns. One of her earthly concerns was me, and I would lose her, sometimes for many months at a time.

As a child, I'd needed my mother to be reliable, but I'd had to give up the idea that I could depend on her. I didn't analyse the situation, I simply concluded that she probably didn't like me, or maybe didn't really love me, though she said she did. I became conditioned to feelings of disappointment, pain, fear and anger. It became my "normal". I swallowed my feelings, unable to speak up in defence of my own needs in any way. Now, pushing the lawnmower along, I could sense something wrapping itself around my heart and lighting up in my mind. I could feel the distress as though I suddenly had access to my child-self. I was on high alert just as I had been all those years ago. The feeling of panic was visceral. I understood that this scene was a replay of something that had felt horrendous – life-threatening, whether or not that was actually, *literally* so. But I had not fought for my life then or even explained how frightened or hurt I felt.

A strand of history was repeating itself. I was on the outside while Gerald got all of the pie. She was an adult. I was an adult, so in a way that didn't matter. Now, surely, I *could* speak because I was an adult. Now perhaps I *had* to speak if I wanted to heal the wound that clearly still existed. But how could I when, in a way, it was none of my business what my elderly mother did? She was no longer playing the role of parent and I was no longer the vulnerable child. Or was I?

Even at this late stage in our life together I wanted to change things. It didn't seem healthy to let it fester unexpressed, yet my rational mind only led me into cul-de-sacs when I tried to work out how to do it. Old trauma had been triggered, ignited, brought into the light of the present, and I wasn't sure I was up to the job of handling it.

I didn't yearn to be the apple of Mum's eye, or to be indispensable, or the most important person in her life. But I didn't want to be cast aside either. There were two forces working against this. One was my mother's old pattern of losing herself completely in a man, the other was Gerald himself, who seemed to be monopolising Mum's time and energy and influencing her in a way that pushed me out into the cold.

It seemed I was powerless. Admitting that I felt hurt would surely leave me in a very vulnerable place. In a contest for my mother's love, I was certain I would lose to the paramour and the knowledge of that fact silenced me. It made me complicit in playing a game of "let's pretend" in which nobody said anything and we all continued acting out our roles.

My mother had finally lost control of her emotions and I couldn't find the words to defend myself against the power of her eruptions or simply tell the truth about how I felt: that being pushed away one minute and pulled in to support her the next was unacceptable to me. There were things I needed to say but simply could not utter. Things like 'Please stop ranting and raving at me! I never signed up to be your unpaid maid, or your lifelong crisis counsellor', and 'I won't allow you to hurt me anymore.'

All I'd managed so far was to suggest some practical steps Mum could take in having more independence, like getting a mobility scooter, and I even heard myself saying, 'You're very lucky, Mum, there are people out there far worse off than you.' This was something I had vowed never to say to my own children.

❧

David and I were happy with our part-time togetherness, which was remarkably similar to the weekend-only pattern of the previous year. One significant difference was that we were no longer completely frazzled. The clincher was that we had the freedom to choose our lifestyle this time. I was benefitting from my weekly retreats in my house, enjoying my time alone. However, even within in the sanctuary of my home, Mum appeared inside my mind a lot of the time. Increasingly my time and energy were taken up with worry about her mental state, and confusion about being an adult re-visiting childhood neglect. She seemed to be disappearing into an emotional whirlpool and I was getting pulled in with her.

I felt we were heading for some kind of crisis and I had to do something. I wondered if I should get professional help for her even though she had refused when I suggested a visit to her doctor. I needed to talk to someone, and I could have shared my concerns with my brother, but Mum had banned me from telling him about the turmoil she was in.

I had been so careful, over the decades, to bury my own store of upsetting memories and feelings. I had found relative peace and gained some control over my life. My mother's re-enactment of the old pattern had blown the lid off. I was frozen, not knowing which path to take. Should I do something to avert disaster or leave her be? And should I get professional help for myself?

⁂

Things came to a head during a forty-minute car journey to one of Mum's hearing-aid appointments. As soon as we were trapped together in the car she started on a rant. She looked crazed. I decided to keep quiet, considering it the best option. I tried to concentrate on the road but she'd really got into the swing of her tantrum and seemed angry that I wouldn't join in. What she was saying made sense linguistically, but it was irrational and, dare I say it, hysterical. It was all about Gerald and the fact that she thought everything had gone wrong with him.

I suggested that she might be seeing things askew: things might be quite a lot less bleak than she thought and she might have jumped to unrealistic conclusions. I wanted to reassure her, calm her down, but she assured me she was absolutely right, everything was beyond terrible, and I was wrong to think I knew anything.

I had never seen Mum quite like this before and I was shocked. Maybe she really had lost the plot. Perhaps this was the breakdown she had hitherto managed to avert. I tried to work out what to do. I went back to staying silent and hummed almost inaudibly to myself. At the same time I continued to read the road and try to work out what to do next. Somehow I had to manage her physically and get her to an appointment that now seemed irrelevant and inappropriate. After that, assuming we survived the journey home, perhaps I needed to get help immediately.

Getting Mum from car to wheelchair and vice versa was challenging at the best of times. On this occasion, just as we were negotiating the risky, pivotal point in the manoeuvre, Mum said she felt like giving up. Not just on the task in hand but on life. She seemed exhausted, weak and distressed and she appeared to be about to throw herself to the ground. I gave her a verbal slap in the face and shouted, telling her to pull herself together. I had to.

The slap seemed to work. She rallied a little, and, miraculously, we rolled into the clinic looking fairly normal, I thought. The handsome audiologist ushered us into his office. I left her there, saying I would collect her in half an hour, as usual. I went into a nearby store for some emergency retail therapy though my mind was not really on the job. My heart was pounding, there was a dull rushing sound in my ears and my mind felt numb.

When I returned Mum was sitting in the hallway outside the office, beaming and chuckling. 'What a nice man! What a charming chap. We had such a giggle together,' she gushed. She was completely calm. How could she switch like that? Was it all an act? I was unable to speak and felt frozen with a rage I had to fight to control...

I realised while driving home to David's that I had reached the end of my rope. I was shaking with fury and stress. Mum seemed like a different person from the woman I'd cared for six months before and I was already dreading my next visit.

Though Mum had forbidden me, as soon as I got home I phoned my brother. Telling the story of our desperate car journey to someone far away from the day-to-day theatricals was surprisingly helpful. My brother laughed. Through his eyes I could see that the situation was ludicrous – a farce. I laughed too and it was a huge relief.

He sympathised about the stress I was feeling. I told him of my concerns about Mum's mental state and about Gerald. 'I'll go and visit this weekend,' he said. I had spilled Mum's beans and that felt bad, but I needed my brother to be on board from now on.

⁂

My brother rang for a de-brief. He had seen what I had seen. He'd spent an afternoon with someone who physically resembled our mother but, he said, he did not recognise this woman. He felt confused and decidedly uncomfortable, but she had at least seemed happy, smiling and flirting. I realised as the conversation unfolded that Gerald had been present, and he had been charming, if a little odd.

I felt calm as I walked into Mum's flat. I put the laundry on, emptied the bins and cleaned the bathroom. Mum seemed peaceful and cheery. We talked about practical things and I told her I was now actively looking for a carer for her, which met with approval. We got on to the subject of how she was. 'Oh, I'm fine,' she breezed. Was this cheeriness what she had meant when she'd bragged about her poker face? Had her meltdown happened only in my imagination? There was no disharmony today, no drama. I could either leave, having experienced a rather pleasant whitewash, or I'd have to initiate something.

'Mum, I have to tell you I am no longer willing to be your emotional repository,' I said.

'I know I've been upset lately but you can understand what it's like for me...' she replied.

'Yes,' I told her. 'I understand, and I am saying that I am not willing to be your sounding board.'

'But who else can I tell? I haven't got any friends, it's not my fault.'

'I see your problem and I am sorry about it, but I am not willing to be your emotional dustbin. You'll have to find another solution.'

'I have to talk to *someone*, I've had a lot...'

'I understand, but *I* am not willing...'

'But you can just let it flow over you. Don't let it get to you.'

'Mum!' I raised my voice. 'I don't want you to dump your emotional crap on me anymore, okay?'

There was a long silence. Was she going to cry, get angry or drop dead? I didn't know. Eventually she said, 'I see. Yes. Heard and understood.' Another silence followed, then, 'Gosh! I don't want you to dread coming to see me.'

'No more outpourings, okay?'

'Okay,' she concluded, looking a little cowed. We'd got there in the end thanks to a standard assertiveness technique I'd learned in the nineties.

Before I left I suddenly thought of something. 'How did you manage when you lived alone? I only saw you every few months,' I asked.

She thought for a while then said gloomily, 'I don't know. It was different.'

Then it came to me.

'You used to write. You wrote every single day. Now you don't write at all.'

'My God!' She seemed genuinely shocked. 'I haven't written for eighteen months.'

'Well, maybe it's time to start again,' I said.

There was another silence during which something seemed to expand into the room like a bright mist. 'Writing was my friend. I'd forgotten,' she said, staring into a memory.

As we said goodbye I hugged her tightly and felt genuine compassion for the first time in a while. I felt I had been heard. I no longer felt small and squashed.

❧

Next time I visited, Mum seemed to have rebooted herself and rewritten her inner programme, deleting things like moaning and complaining, along with anything negative or melodramatic, and replacing them with positive comments about her view and the weather, and brief references to Gerald of an optimistic nature. Evidently she was able to switch programmes very easily, which was fascinating and slightly annoying.

It appeared that she had also installed a new self-management programme. She told me, 'I need very little help these days, thank you very much. Gerald has offered to organise my shopping and push my wheelchair to the surgery.' She seemed supremely confident all of a sudden.

She no longer wanted my suggestions or opinions either, she said, because she found them 'unhelpful'. I apologised for giving unsolicited advice, adding, 'So, I don't need to worry about you then. You are perfectly capable of running your life. That's good.' But I wondered if Mum was reacting to what she perceived as a rejection or a telling off. Was she shutting me out because I had stood up for myself?

What might have seemed like a very small step on my part was actually crucial. I had found myself at the pivotal point around which our relationship revolved. It had taken me a very long time but I had finally come to understand a bit about how Mum worked. There would be no more pussyfooting around what I had perceived as her fragility. Her drama queen strategy – whether conscious or unconscious – was not going to work for her any more now that I had named it. But how was I going to feel now that she was pushing me away?

Life went on. Mum was polite and frosty. There was a lull: an opportunity to focus on my own projects. Then came the run-up to the general election. Mum said her postal voting card had arrived and that she would be voting Conservative. Seeing the look on my face she said, 'I know how you feel and there's no point in us talking.' I was shocked because she had often expressed her disgust at the Tory's policies and various scandals. Mum seemed to have made a radical turnabout and I couldn't help thinking that Gerald had influenced her, though, strangely, she had barely mentioned him for some time.

'Why have you changed…' I asked.

'I'm not discussing it,' she cut in coldly, avoiding eye contact. 'We'll have to agree to disagree on this.'

A few days later she gave me her letters to post and among them was her postal vote. I had been entrusted with this important document, and one which I felt was against my principles to post.

It was the bank holiday weekend, so I left the letters in my car while I spent a few days socialising with David and other friends. I asked a few of them what they would do in my shoes and the responses varied. Some said they'd burn it, others suggested changing her vote, others still said that posting it was the only right thing to do. None of these solutions felt right to me. She had placed her trust in me, not imagining for a second that I would stoop so low as to betray it. She was right: I wouldn't burn it, but I found myself in a dilemma.

After a good night's sleep I knew what to do. I felt at peace when I went to see her later. I handed her the envelope. 'In all conscience I cannot play a part, however peripheral, in helping secure this government's future,' I told her. 'That would jar with my moral principles. I'm not religious, as you know, but I am a big fan of what I consider to be the true essence of Christ's teachings, and those teachings are in direct conflict with the greed, dishonesty and lack of compassion that are displayed continuously by the government under which we suffer at this time.' I was quite pleased with my little speech and thought that her Christian leanings would be in harmony with my point.

She looked horrified. 'Well, I think that's *terrible*!' she exclaimed.

'I could have burned it or binned it, but I returned it. You'll have to get someone else to post it,' I said.

'Burned it? That would have been wicked,' she shrieked, shooting me a quick thunderous look then turning away to study a hairgrip with great intensity.

'I agree, that would have been wicked. Still, I have to do what's right for me,' I said.

'But had our positions been reversed I would have posted *your* vote, whoever you voted for,' she said stiffly. I felt suddenly nervous and thought she was about to banish me from her flat.

'Mum, I really wanted to talk about it before, but you refused and...'

'I know what you think,' she cut in, sharply.

'Maybe you don't know what I think. I just wanted to understand why you've changed...' At that moment there was a knock on the door and Mum wafted past to welcome Gerald with a huge smile. I said hello to him and goodbye to my mother, and left with the feeling that Mum had already forgotten I was still there in the room.

Driving home, I felt sad that Mum and I couldn't talk about our political differences and hear each other's views. Perhaps I'd been petty and my speech a little pompous, but I was puzzled that she'd made such a U-turn from the way she had been talking only a year before. I was hurt that she seemed so hostile. My stomach was in a knot.

Mum emailed me later and I thought she was going to tear me off a strip for not doing things in the way that she would have done them; for being cruel or overly principled. But she just thanked me politely for my work and went on to describe the weather and what she'd eaten for supper. A perfectly bland email.

⁂

My mother was very excited when her new carer visited for the first time. I was running late and arrived to find them already engaged in convivial conversation. Mum was animated, showing off a little bit. The carer, Audrey, seemed lovely and very suitable. I could imagine them getting on famously. At one point, Mum was explaining something to Audrey and waved her hand extravagantly in my direction, saying, 'We've got things running pretty smoothly here, haven't we *darling*?' I was amazed and felt slightly uncomfortable. I didn't remember her ever calling me darling like that. It was as though I had a different mother all of a sudden.

⁂

Mum had had a visit from my daughter, who later told me that her grandmother had talked coherently, not darting about from topic to topic like a crazy fish. I visited as usual and this time felt softer towards her. She seemed more herself, the self that I think of as her usual default self: not too confrontational, not too negative, not overexcited; just kind of normal. I wondered whether she considered that she had shown me enough of her cold shoulder and moved on. Her new carer, Audrey, was working out well.

One Sunday she had a severe nosebleed that wouldn't stop,

and texted to say that she needed me to clean up her flat. When I got there it looked like a crime scene. I took care of her while she recovered her strength.

The next day I took Mum to the doctor, who couldn't find any cause for concern. On Thursday I visited her again and delivered the shopping she'd asked for. She was cheerful. 'You can forget all about me for a while. I am really happy and I can manage well with a little help from Audrey,' she said.

On Saturday morning I received an email. 'We don't seem to be in touch very much these days,' Mum complained. I was astonished. I visited again a few days later and she told me that she had no recollection of any of the things she'd said over the past week. She didn't even remember that I had been there on three days out of five.

Something seemed to be happening, and happening rather swiftly. Most of the time, Mum forgot almost everything that had gone before, except things she had learned at school and stories from her earlier life, many of which she recounted repeatedly, forgetting that she had already told them to me.

She seemed terribly confused as well as forgetful – she couldn't help it. I knew I had to be firm and assertive with her regarding my boundaries. At the same time, I could see that I had to support her in preserving whatever orderliness of mind she had available. I suggested that a memory board might help her to stay with the programme.

I knew that her sudden decline had something to do with the considerable turbulence that seemed to revolve around Gerald. Now she didn't emote about him to me, but spoke in a matter-of-fact way that made it clear that he was the decision maker in the relationship and that he was a fixture. Mum saw herself as independent again – the elder of the family who didn't need me to play a parental role with her, yet we were all under Gerald's thumb because she completely submitted to him and expected me not to argue with her. I was in danger of finding myself back in my place: a child, seen and not heard.

Audrey was able to clean and do a bit of shopping but, ultimately, the responsibility for Mum's wellbeing sat on my shoulders, whether I wanted that or not. I hoped I had learned my lesson over the recent months: I didn't want to sacrifice myself and my life any longer. But I couldn't abandon her if she was losing her mind. More than anything, I felt I ought to keep an eye on the Gerald situation. All this thinking and worrying filled my time and left me exhausted.

❦

Back at home, the house was quiet. I unpacked the car, showered, ate and slept. I woke up feeling a strange and sudden emptiness. I wondered what I was doing there. It dawned on me that all the silence and solitude I had indulged in for the first few months of the year had done their work. I had been emptied out and filled up. I'd done enough retreating. I had reset my relationship with my mother as much as that was possible.

Now I was ready to do other things – have some fun. After all, it was the summer holidays, despite the atrocious August weather. To continue with my routines of toing and froing – though it had suited me for a while – suddenly seemed pointless. Something had been stopping me from seeing this before.

It was as though I was trapped in carer-mode. Even though Mum had moved on and told me in no uncertain terms that she intended to manage her life by herself, she was still pulling my strings. I was on call, on hold and weighed down with responsibility. I rarely allowed myself to have a laugh or a dance, or anything else that was just for me.

It was time I got myself together, shook out my swimsuit and let my hair down. I decided to go on holiday. Mum had Audrey and Gerald. It would be fine. It all made perfect sense suddenly.

I packed up all the stuff that I had unpacked the evening before and drove to my mother's flat. I suggested she use her notice board to help her remember all the little things that kept falling through the cracks. She liked the idea and got started right away. I was about to tell her that I would be out of service for a while. 'I've been thinking,' she announced. 'It's time you had a proper break.'

It seemed her memory was faulty but her psychic powers were red hot. 'Funny you should mention that,' I said, and I told her I would be on holiday for a fortnight.

I hugged her, saying, 'See you in a couple of weeks then.'

'Oh, are you going somewhere?' she asked.

'Yes, I am on holiday from today, I just told you,' I said with mild exasperation.

'Oh yes, that's right. I'll write it down. Where did I put my notice board?' She found it and then asked, 'What am I writing down?'

I left her beaming and telling me that she felt at home now in her flat, the one that God had forgotten. She seemed to be losing her mind, yet she seemed happy, or perhaps she was simply relieved that I would be out of the way for a while.

❧

I settled myself in at David's, which was my home too, except that I had not moved back in full-time since I left to care for

Mum twenty months before. He was quietly happy to have me there buying groceries and cooking, though he'd never say such a thing. He tended to get a bit lost on his own, and I was beginning to realise that I did too.

I was enjoying my holiday. I'd given myself permission not to jump to attention in response to requests or demands in the form of texts and emails. No demands came. It seemed that my mother had remembered that I was taking a break. This seemed miraculous. I visited my daughter and we had lunch in a café surrounded by holiday makers who were sheltering from the awful weather and consoling themselves with good food.

One day the rain was unrelenting. There was no possibility of a walk so I stayed in bed, thinking and listening. There was only a skylight between me and the un-forecast deluge. I thought about all those families enduring their holidays in soggy, sagging tents. I drifted into a reverie of my own childhood holidays on the Pembrokeshire coast, where I had spent a dozen Augusts with the same four people in the same tiny caravan and awning.

We were rarely bored back then. We were drenched, web-footed, mouldering, cabin-fevered, heavy with longing and frustrated, but we were not bored. Watching the sky for a break in the cloud we would sit and play cards and board games and tune Mum's radio to Radio One when she was somewhere else. Where did she go for shelter from the long holidays that we so loved, but that she only tolerated?

Sometimes a storm would last for days. I remember wearing a long mac over my beloved bikini and feeling the clammy interior meld to my skin. It was wellies or flip-flops depending on the temperature of the day. Mostly it was warm enough for a sea-swim in the rain, after which it was impossible to get dry. I'd walk back to the caravan soaked with a mixture of salt and fresh water. If I was neglected – and I guess I was, relatively speaking: an orphan while my parents went sailing whatever the weather – I never *felt* neglected on holiday because the last thing I wanted was parental attention, or a bath or a trip to a funfair, or a museum or something edifying like that. I was in my element in my salad days in August in Pembrokeshire. I was in heaven.

My mother said the sea would keep us clean but she would insist I had a proper wash at least once per holiday. She half-filled a faded red bowl with kettle-warmed water and coached me. 'Dip the flannel in the bowl and wash your face and neck. Dip again and do your arms, back and front. Sit in the bowl and deal with the important bits. Now stand in it and get the mud off your feet. Chuck the filthy water in the hedge.'

Mackerel were plentiful and easy to catch. Lobsters and crabs were on the menu. On the double gas ring my mother cooked family meals and we all crammed round the little table which was designed for four average people. There was very little elbow room and there were fights. When my dad was with us for his two-week holiday, he put a total ban on arguing at the table and so my brothers would glare silently at one another with scowls and body language that said *We'll sort this out later*. And they did, but the worst of their battles were fought back at home. On one occasion, they violently reorganised the kitchen and my parents came home to what looked like the aftermath of a Greek wedding. That went down in our family history. But holidays in Pembrokeshire, whether soggy or gloriously baking hot, were far too precious to be squandered on fraternal warfare, so mostly we all got along. After dinner, we took it in turns to wash the dishes in the faded red bowl.

I discovered much later that my mother only tolerated our magical holidays. I was shocked. I had assumed she was as crazily in love with the place as I was. How could anyone not be? But for her it was a sacrifice. She loved the view but felt like an outsider – lonely. Mum facilitated our enjoyment by sticking around, at least at mealtimes and bedtimes, while my father returned to work having driven with my brothers in his estate car down the A48, through the traffic jams of Carmarthen and along the hilly, twisting A and B roads that led to our own personal paradise. He towed the touring caravan which was packed with all our stuff. On his roof-rack was a Mirror dinghy. My mum's Hillman Imp, carrying me and towing a sleek racing boat, completed the convoy. Dad would settle us in then return to the world of black and white, roads and buildings, profits and losses, to keep his business afloat while we revelled in the ecstatic, technicolour experience of west Wales in full holiday swing.

When he returned two weeks later for his holiday, I would almost burst with excitement. I adored my Holiday Dad who was relaxed, tanned and lots of fun. There would be treats, and despite the sailing schedule that was hugely important to my parents, there would be time for the wonderful things that we always did on holiday. We would walk the coast path that snaked round the headland, we'd go to pubs for pasties and Coke, we'd play French cricket, spend a day cooking sausages at a secret beach, and eat fish and chips on the harbour wall on the way home. These were fairly ordinary things, but they sparkled with magic because we were a family together on holiday.

❦

My self-styled staycation was over and I visited Mum. She seemed to have taken on board that I was not her companion, her counsellor or her emotional dustbin. And she had managed perfectly well without me for two weeks which boded well for my upcoming trip with David. Unusually, we played Scrabble. Though Mum was a little frosty and carefully polite, it was a satisfactory visit and a sticky game, which was better than the other way round.

During my next visit Mum told me she and Gerald were planning to visit some old friends in Yorkshire. I was astonished. Her proposed holiday was going to take place while David and I were away on our long-postponed trip to Portugal. Gerald was not in the best of health and could only walk with sticks. He hadn't driven for months yet they were planning to go off in his small, battered car to the north of England in the middle of winter and I wouldn't be in the country to help them in any way. She had barely left the confines of the building during the year she had lived there.

I was concerned about the unpredictable weather, the shortness of the days and the fact that Mum would need physical help that Gerald would not be able to give her. Gerald sounded, from what she had told me, to be not only bossy but unrealistic in his assessment of his own, and my mother's, abilities. He was very ambitious for her. I was alarmed that she was planning to put her life in the hands of a man she found it impossible to reason with or stand up to.

I felt that if they wanted to go on a holiday they needed a bit of support, clement weather and an appropriate vehicle that could take all Mum's mobility aids. I was impressed by her adventurous spirit, but an image was forming in my mind of two elderly disabled people stuck in a snow drift, in the dark, in the cold north. I voiced my concerns.

'*You're* going off on a trip, why shouldn't *I*?' she said, petulantly. 'It might be my last chance to have an adventure. Why would you deny me that?'

I could see that Mum really wanted to visit her friends, who were keen to meet the man they had heard so much about in Mum's letters. I could also see that I was being protective – a spoilsport – but I thought my uneasiness was valid.

Mum had implied on several occasions that Gerald had taken complete control over her life and now it seemed a battle had begun. Could it be, I wondered, that despite her fantasy about driving off into the gloom with Gerald, she was covertly crying for help, and hoping I would stop her?

I could simply let go and walk away, but I wasn't sure that was really the right thing to do, even if it suited me to some extent. I tried again to suggest they hold off until I returned from my trip; then it would be spring, and I would at least be around to help or rescue them.

'It might be a pipe dream,' said Mum. 'It might never happen, so why worry?'

She was right; it might have been a pipe dream, but that didn't take away the worry. I realised that Mum had truly lost herself in Gerald. He must have looked to her like the lead in a romantic novel, turning up and sweeping her off her feet. Mum had never been particularly grounded but now it seemed she was caught up in a complete fantasy world.

Mum would say, 'Gerald has decided this; Gerald wants me to do that; Gerald drinks like a fish,' and, 'I am under his spell; I don't have a say in things; it's easier if I just go along with it; that's just the way it is.' I began to feel deeply suspicious of Gerald.

'So let me get this right,' I said. 'You see that Gerald is domineering and a bit of a control freak and you can't stand up to him, but you are okay with that?'

'Yes,' she replied.

'And you want me to back off and leave you to live your life as you see fit?'

'Yes. That's right,' she said emphatically. I couldn't be sure whether she genuinely felt this way or whether Gerald had insisted she got me off their backs.

'That's fine,' I said, 'but it puts me in a difficult position because I have a duty of care towards you and I need to know you are not being bullied.'

'Yes, I see that. I am being pulled from both sides and I am stuck in the middle.' There was a pause then she added levelly, 'Being with Gerald is my choice. It is not negotiable. I have chosen *him*. I just want you to leave me alone to mess my life up if that's what I am going to do.' The discussion was finished, it seemed.

❧

It was just a few weeks until we were due to leave for our trip. We had been waiting for a long, long time and a lot had changed in the two years since we had made the decision to go. I talked to Mum again about her proposed holiday in Yorkshire.

'I never said I was going while you were away. Where did you get that idea?' she said, sounding indignant. I was relieved and decided not to argue about the details of our previous conversations on the subject. Mum also told me she felt fine about me being away, especially as my daughter and my brother were going to be stepping in to support her when needed. That was another relief. And of course Gerald would be around, that was a given. 'And you have Audrey too,' I reminded her. But apparently Audrey had stopped coming. Mum was not exactly evasive, but she had no explanation as to why.

On Christmas Eve we celebrated the festive season with Mum and my brother over dinner in her flat. 'Gerald has decided not to join us as he has taken offence over your attitude towards our trip to Yorkshire,' Mum said in a voice that told me she had also taken umbrage with me. On Christmas Day David and I huddled up in his motor home at the beach, sheltering from horizontal rain and gales. I felt defeated and deflated.

We'd booked our ferry tickets and were now committed to setting out on our journey in the New Year. We both felt unsure whether we wanted to go any more. The two-year postponement had taken the edge off our appetites for adventure and brought on a feeling of inertia. Excitement had been replaced by worry and apprehension.

❧

It was April, three months since we had set out on our journey to Portugal the slow way. We had made it back home to Wales after a very challenging final week during which a tyre exploded as we drove at high speed (for us) along a motorway in Spain. We felt lucky to have survived.

It was hard to think about the entire trip now that it had been eclipsed by this traumatic end. We agreed that it hadn't been quite the escape from reality we might have been hoping for. Had it been worth waiting for? I wondered. Had it all been worth the cost, which had less to do with money and more to do with stress and challenge, and expenditure of energy and time?

Before we set off, I'd felt as though I was fighting for my life. Not life as opposed to death, but life in the sense of freedom. I had been holding too many feelings. I felt like a balloon that was about to explode. Then, somewhere along the road, the stress dissipated. When I thought about the distant past there was nothing there to hold onto. I tried not to think about my mother.

Three weeks into our voyage I had received an email. 'Bad news' it stated. Mum went on to tell me that she had gone to Gerald's flat and found him dead on the floor. My heart went out to her immediately. I knew that he was everything to her and that she had modelled her new life around him. She had expected to meet death pretty soon but hadn't expected it to visit Gerald. She was devastated by the loss and traumatised by the horrible discovery. I began to think about getting back home as quickly as possible to comfort her and take care of things. I phoned my brother who told me to stay put. He and my daughter would look after Mum. 'You've done your share,' he said. I emailed or spoke to Mum most days. She said it was helpful to talk. She was desperately sad but she sounded incredibly strong, as she had always been in a crisis. Yet again she had lost the man in her life.

Grievances and misgivings were irrelevant now and the feelings I'd had about Gerald just ebbed away. I felt for my mum in her time of loss and grief. There was nothing I could do from Portugal and really there was nothing to be done anyway. Mum just needed to pour out her heart and I was happy to listen.

Evidently, after Gerald's death, all the other residents had started gathering round Mum and offering condolences and support. They were extremely kind and understanding. Over many months they had witnessed an exclusive bubble forming around Gerald and Mum and they recognised that these two people were forming a deep bond. They cared. They seemed to like my mum and she started to reach out to them in a way she never had before.

It took a few days for us to land and settle at home. I went to visit Mum as soon as I could. She was delighted to see me and wanted to tell the story that she had kept to herself until I came home. She talked for a long time, detailing the dreadful discovery.

She reiterated her assertion that Gerald had been a difficult and damaged person and then she told me that when she had seen him that very first time, across the dining hall, she had known that he needed her and that her job would be to help him in some way. She hadn't understood it at the time but she knew it had something to do with love.

Gerald was a proud man, substantial in physique and strong in will. He had been successful in all areas of his life with the exception of human relations. Love was something he had never been able to receive. In childhood his relationship with his mother had been a living nightmare and he had never held onto a relationship in his adult life, not even with his only son, from whom he had become estranged.

Mum had discovered all this over the course of a year. At first he had been secretive but later he had come to trust her. Finally he told her his entire, unedited life story. She was his only confidante and once he had started to share his feelings with her he couldn't stop. She didn't mind, she told me. She loved him in a way that had shocked her. This love was deep and all-consuming.

During the last few weeks of his life Gerald couldn't bear to be apart from Mum. Something was happening to him. 'He was transformed,' she said. 'He became soft and sweet and loving. He might have known he didn't have long, but he never expressed that. I think he was scared but eventually he gave up trying to hold onto control over his destiny. In those last weeks he became humble. He was just open and full of love.'

She continued. 'Not everyone liked Gerald. Some people actively disliked him. I knew that. But he had sought me out – me of all people! I was old enough to be his mother. He showed me how vulnerable he really was. He hid nothing from me. He leant on me and looked to me for solace. Towards the end he simply melted.'

Gerald had been aware that he was ill and that he was not meant to touch alcohol at all, but he had taken up drinking with great enthusiasm and in large quantities. Perhaps he had given up fighting to survive. He had found someone to love who loved him back unconditionally and with great force, like a mother.

I was one of the people who had found Gerald difficult. I

had seen his increasing influence on my mother and the resultant change in her character. That didn't matter now. I was hearing a testimony about the transformation of a person who had found a safe haven for his soul at the end of his road. It struck me as ironic that my mother, who had often been unable to play a supportive maternal role with me, had been so willing and able to offer refuge to Gerald.

I wondered what would happen next: whether my mother would return to normal, though I had no idea what "normal" meant in relation to my mother. Losing her beloved friend, and particularly discovering his lifeless body, had left her shattered. She was changed by the experience. She was grieving, properly. She even started seeing a bereavement counsellor on the advice of her doctor. She seemed open, soft and wistful, profoundly sad and remarkably strong all at the same time. She had hit bedrock and now a more authentic self was exposed. Perhaps this was her real self, which had been hidden beneath the layers of her personality that had sometimes confused and frustrated me.

❧

One day during her gradual recovery from the acute phase of her bereavement, Mum informed me that Gerald hadn't liked me and had wanted me out of the way because he had desired to have control of her and possess her. She said this as though she was telling me about Gerald's choice in football teams or music, and I wondered if she realised that I had been feeling increasingly alienated from her over the months. It felt as though my position in her life had been under threat, despite the fact that Mum had always said that she had unconditional love for all her children – always had and always would.

Her dedication to a man who didn't like me and wanted me out of the picture was very upsetting to hear about. It implied that when push came to shove her loyalty leaned toward him and, as she had said, he was a very difficult man. She might have thought she could handle conflicts of interest that would inevitably arise, but I was not so sure.

Had Gerald still been around, especially after my three-month absence, it might have been very difficult for Mum to be genuinely close to us both. Over the year that Mum knew him she had taken a path that, had its trajectory continued, might well have arrived at a distressing impasse – something that we had been spared.

It was easier to be around Mum after her loss. This was partly due to the change in her – she was warm and friendly again, sincerely appreciating my presence – and it was also due to a subtle yet fundamental change that had occurred in me and been absorbed while I was travelling, far away from Mum. I felt free at last to visit her and help her out without feeling trapped in our roles. I had looked at our relationship and seen her from the outside with my own adult eyes, rather than from a place in my psyche that was shared with her, part of her.

I had come to terms with the facts of the matter; come to accept my mother and let go of ideas I'd had about how she "should" be – how I wished her to be.

There had been a unique pattern – a network of pathways – that existed between us. It had seemed fixed only because we held its shape for it. While refusing to face it and continuing with a set of habits that interlocked, we made the pattern seem like a real thing. Perhaps there had been a degree of comfort in the familiarity of the old shape, but it wasn't real and it had no actual power of its own.

To some extent I'd identified and dismantled my part of

our shared pattern. It had been frightening and uncomfortable to break it apart but I had to fight my way out of our dynamic for the sake of both of us. Mum might not even have been aware of the dissolving of our historical relationship and that didn't matter. I had disentangled myself from the unseen ties that bound me to her. Being an adult carer of my elderly mother had given me the opportunity to face and clean up some lifelong wounds. For that I was truly grateful.

Epilogue

Around six months after Gerald's death Mum said that she felt her period of mourning had come to a natural end. She still thought about him every day but no longer felt depressed and paralysed by grief. Her health was generally good but her legs had become weaker than ever, so we finally bought a mobility scooter, which she loved. Her sense of humour had returned and she had managed to regain some faith in her inner guiding voice. God had come home to her – or she had come home to God. Either way she had found peace. Her memory was a little unreliable, but her mood was stable, sunny and relaxed. She seemed happier than I had seen her for years – possibly ever. I continued to visit her once a week, which was a pleasure and which suited us both. She had a busy schedule as she had made friends with a few of her neighbours.

During the year my mother and I lived together I had started writing a journal. It started out as nothing more than notes jotted down in snatched moments. I found it therapeutic to write about the experience, to get it off my chest. Writing kept me sane.

Once she had moved into her own flat I thought I would have nothing more to say on the subject of our journey together. It was over. I didn't know what Gerald would bring into our lives.

When she lived under his spell, though largely independent in her flat, Mum was just as present in my life and in my mind as she had been in the previous year. I had more time to myself and that gave me space to sift through the feelings, look at all that had happened and all that had not happened; we had unfinished business, it turned out.

It was only once there was a safe distance between our homes that I could gain perspective, confront our issues and finally stand up for myself. I had made some headway in letting her know how I felt. Looking back, I was not sure what I had been afraid of exactly. But I had been afraid. If things had gone badly wrong at least I was no longer living with the enemy, so to speak. I could retreat to my sanctuary.

Later, after Gerald died, I found myself in a new place with Mum. She wasn't pulling any strings. Perhaps neither of us had to play the role of parent any longer. This was a comfortable place for me to be. This was my favourite mother.

Whenever we got onto the subject of her year with Gerald she smiled and feasted on happy memories. On one occasion I remarked, not unsympathetically, that it had been a very fraught period and that she had been profoundly distressed at times. 'Yes, that's what love does to a person,' she said authoritatively. I said nothing. We clearly had different ideas about love. That year had been difficult and painful for me but it was over and now it was just a story – a strange love story, perhaps.

One afternoon we were talking about life in general and how culture had changed over the decades since she married my dad. Suddenly Mum said, 'You were such a beautiful baby. You were unplanned but very, very welcome.' Then she looked at me steadily and added, 'I know I let you down. I wasn't there for you. I can't talk about it. It's just too painful. I can't change the past.'

'It's okay,' I said. 'We don't need to go there.'

❧

It was November and nearly three years since my mother collapsed and came to live with me. I decided to make Christmas puddings using my gran's recipe. As Granny mixed the ingredients in her huge bowl, she would make wishes for her family and stir them all into the mixture. I stirred and wished, and my heart swelled with love for my grandmother.

I thought of Mum too. A long time ago I had painted a portrait of her. It contained a lot of shadow and shade and it had been drawn from a narrow angle. The observations were not necessarily inaccurate, but they were only a fine sliver – a troubled daughter's perspective – a view from inside the dynamic.

My portrait of myself was also distorted. There was a part of myself that I had never been able to live with comfortably. I abandoned it, tried to push it away out of sight. It had to do with heredity – the fact that I came from a mother I could not accept fully.

Failing to be honest about ourselves and our vulnerabilities was something we had always done in our family and in our culture. I had played the game that was expected of me for fear of finding myself left out in the cold, alone.

Circumstances had thrown Mum and me together; pushed us to our limits and forced us into a process. We had been given the gift of no escape. When my back was against the wall I stopped playing the game. I no longer cared if I disappointed Mum or anyone else. I realised how toxic it had been for me to protect my mother's pride and position, rather than tell the truth. I had heard my younger self call to me, watched as she showed me where the wound still existed. However modestly, I stood up in defence of her, releasing us from the prison of manners. In the end, the truth set me free from that particular noose.

Mum might have been looking for an escape route too – an escape from the predictable and the inevitable. She bet all her money on one horse and rode off with a handsome stranger, possibly reckoning that he would accompany her to the end of the road. She was willing to risk our relationship. She didn't mind disappointing me.

The diversion certainly took her out of herself. Probably, it took her to a place that she had believed she would never visit again. It might have felt familiar, but the terrain was tougher than it had seemed when she was young and robust. It took its toll on her and then things took a sharp, unexpected turn. She was thrown back on her own reduced resources. Grief stripped away her remaining layers of protection.

Meanwhile, I had come to understand my mother as a whole woman whose life started before I came along. I could see how her life had moulded her into the person she became and driven her to choose the paths she chose. I had a new portrait of her that was broader and more real. It included shadows but it also contained light, love, good memories, valuable lessons she had taught me and all that she had inspired in me. It contained complexities and paradox. I was able, at last, to look at the ways in which she had encouraged me. Seeing her in perspective made it possible to accept her and support her. I could embrace her and embrace the part of me that was made of her. My new self-portrait depicted a woman who was able to move beyond pain, drop expectations and enjoy what it was possible to share: humour, intelligent conversation, company and the genuine love that was at the core of the bond.

※

The next time I visited we talked about writing. I'd urged Mum to get her keyboard out again and she said she had been thinking of some new ideas, though she wasn't feeling very motivated. I mentioned my memoir and told her a lot about the content. She listened with interest. It felt natural to ask if she would like to read it. 'Yes of course I would. I love your writing. You have inherited my writing genes and that makes me happy. I am very proud of you,' she replied. I felt fine a few days later as I printed out my latest draft. I was relaxed as I dropped it off at her flat for her perusal.

That evening I remembered something: a friend from long ago had been in a therapy session where she was encouraged to write a letter that would contain all the things she had never been able to say to her mother, including a list of all the ways in which her mother had failed her. The idea was to write it, burn it and, after the catharsis, move on.

She got into the spirit of the activity and really let rip, pouring out all that she had kept inside: material that had damaged her and poisoned her adult life. It was a long, long letter.

Some days after the workshop she was still in a bit of a strange state and something began to dawn on her. She remembered, now, putting the letter into an envelope, sticking on a stamp and posting it to her mother. My friend was horror-stricken.

※

Every now and then a jolt would pass through me as I remembered that Mum now had my manuscript in her possession. There was no going back. I had jumped out of the aeroplane and I was terrified. What would she think and feel reading my exposé? How could I do such a thing to this elderly and recently bereaved woman? I was shoving in her face things that she knew little about. Was I crazy and self-destructive? Was I massively insensitive or unforgivably cruel?

My heart was pounding as I entered Mum's flat. I spotted the sheaf of paper lying on the sideboard exactly where I had left it. I still had a chance to retrieve it.

'Let's have an oxymoron,' Mum said.

We sat down with the tea just as we always did, and she chatted about her week. 'Did you read my manuscript?' I asked.

'Yes,' she replied.

'And?' I pressed.

'Oh, it's great. *Very* good. Some bits were difficult for me, but overall I enjoyed it. Are you going to publish it?'

I hesitated. 'How would you feel about that?' I asked her. 'Would you be okay with other people reading all that stuff about you?'

'I couldn't care less what anyone thinks about me! Couldn't give a fig,' she said brightly.

I stared at her for a long time.

'Fancy a game of Scrabble?' she asked.

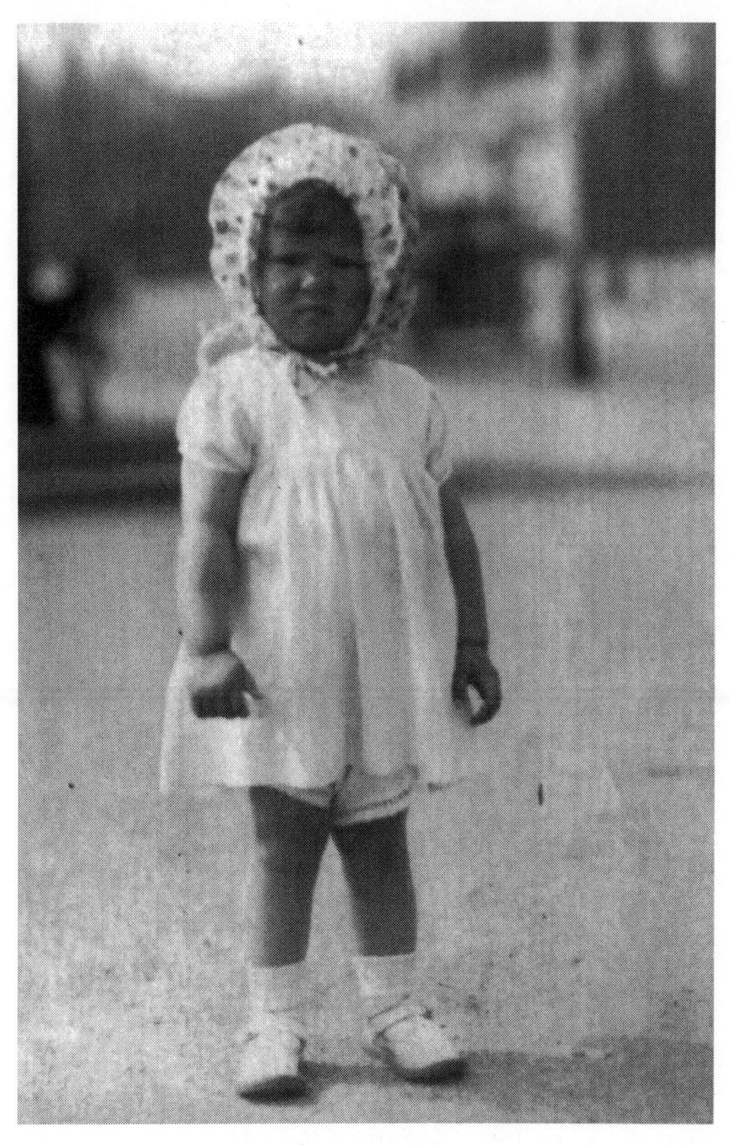

My mum, aged about 2

Acknowledgments

I want to thank the Parthian team for taking on my book and for their brilliant work on its completion.

Especially, I thank Richard Davies for his advice on the early incarnation of my manuscript. I am forever grateful to Carly Holmes for her warm encouragement and sensitive, excellent editing.

Thanks to my small group of readers (friends and family) for their feedback and particularly to Viv Newman who listens so much, so intelligently and so compassionately.

Special thanks go to Dai, who listened actively and endlessly as I read and reread the manuscript. He is also the person who accompanied me through the profoundly challenging episode of my life that prompted me to write the book. I am truly grateful for his forebearance, patience, practical help, loyalty, love and support.

I owe a debt of deep gratitude to Jane and David Shaw. Their incredible skills in empathy and emotional holding, many years ago, enabled me to thrive and start to believe in my self. Without them I doubt I would have written this, or any, book.

Lastly, I thank and honour my mother not only for being a wonderful character to write about but for being extraordinarily open and encouraging about the publication of such an intimate account of our entwined lives. I feel very lucky to have the mum I have, who has inspired in me the things I value most.

A VAN OF ONE'S OWN

BIDDY WELLS

£8.99 | PB
978-1-910901-99-1

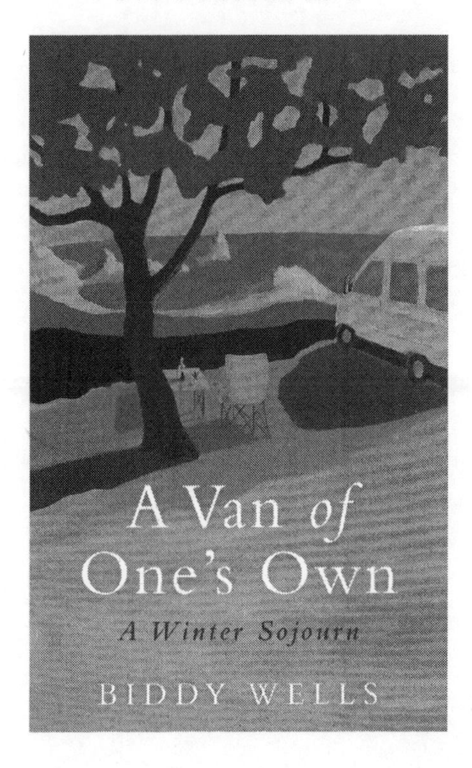

A Van of One's Own is a journey through the breath-taking scenery of France, Spain, and finally Portugal, populated by colourful characters and the roar of the ocean, the taste of fresh fish and the grind of the asphalt; but more importantly, it is a journey through past memories and present conflicts to inner peace.

RIVERWISE:

Meditations On Afon Teifi

JACK SMYLIE WILD

£9.00 | PB

978-1-913640-39-2

Riverwise, a volume of slow river prose centred around Afon Teifi, is a book of wanderings and wonderings, witnessings and enchantments, rememberings and endings. Weaving memoir, poetry and keen observation into its meandering course, it shifts across time and space.

"A lovely book ... Read and enjoy. I certainly did."
Iolo Williams

A WILDER WALES

DAVID LLOYD OWEN

£20.00 | HB

978-1-910901-96-0

David Lloyd Owen introduces us to the fascinating breadth of travellers' tales from a mysterious and absorbing country: writers who described a land of mountains and valleys, ruined castles, and abandoned monasteries.